VITALIZING INTIMACY IN MARRIAGE (VIM)

VITALIZING INTIMACY IN MARRIAGE (VIM)

Patricia Y. Travis
and
Robert P. Travis

Nelson-Hall nh Chicago

Travis, Patricia Y
Vitalizing intimacy in marriage, VIM.

Includes index.
1. Marriage. 2. Sex in marriage.
3. Intimacy (Psychology) I. Travis, Robert P., joint author. II. Title.
HQ734.T82 301.42 79-4374
ISBN 0-88229-398-2

Manufactured in the United States of America

10 9 8 7 6 5 4 3 2 1

Contents

To the many couples who think enough of their marriage to want to make it a better place to live.

Acknowledgments

Although the impetus for VIM came from our own personal and professional interest in marital health, we are deeply indebted to the many hundreds of married partners who participated in our Pairing Enrichment Program—PEP. It was primarily through their enthusiasm of wanting to share PEP with others that this book became a reality.

We also wish to acknowledge Dr. Patrick Linton and Dr. C. J. Rosecrans of the Department of Psychiatry for their encouragement and support and to Ms. Eleanor Beaton for her patience and untiring efforts in typing and retyping the many drafts of the manuscript.

We are particularly indebted to Dr. Clark Vincent for his original ideas and writings on the specialty of Marital Health, the myth of naturalism and other valuable concepts which have served as guiding principles in our own work.

Finally, no writing in the area of marriage enrichment would be complete without acknowledging David and Vera Mace, personal friends and Founders of the Association of Couples for Marriage Enrichment (ACME).

Preface

This book is an exploration into expanding and enriching intimacy between married partners. It is written for couples who want to develop a greater potential for both personal and interpersonal growth *through* their unique marriage relationship. It is for *both* the husband and wife. In this respect it is quite different from the recent outpouring of books directed primarily to the woman who wants to make her man more sensitive, more sensual, more sexual, or to the woman who wants to learn how to control or manipulate her man to get what she wants. We believe the creation of intimacy and its continual growth rests equally with both partners. It does not involve hidden manipulations, but, rather, open communications.

This book is divided into four parts. In Part One we share with you a personal glimpse of the two of us and how this book developed. In Parts Two and Three we attempt to identify some delusions about marriage and about intimacy which we believe blocks the process of vitalizing intimacy in marriage. In these two sections, however, we go beyond just an identification of negatives. We share with you some positive approaches to aid you in your exploration of intensifying the intimate potential of your marriage relationship.

Part Four is a guided exploration of putting the concepts

of Vitalizing Intimacy in Marriage (VIM) into practice for partners who wish to experience these suggestions with each other. We suggest that you do not begin this section until each of you has completed the first three sections.

You may be wondering if this book would be beneficial for couples who are living together but not "married" or for married couples where one partner really wants to expand in intimacy while the other is "satisfied" or sees no point in it.

Let's talk about married vs. nonmarried first. There are probably a lot of good reasons why some people and some couples should not marry. That decision is theirs to make. We, however, have a professional and personal interest in enriching marriages. Almost all of our experience has been in dealing with married couples. We know the changes both positive and negative that can take place in this type of partnership. This book may be helpful in other types of "emerging life styles"—we just don't know. We do know that quite often many attitudes about "appropriate" roles and behaviors change rather dramatically after partners become "legally" married. Because of the sociological, ethical, religious, and legal factors in our culture, marriage is indeed a unique process. We regard it as such.

The second issue can be a real problem. We often see couples where one partner wants more out of the relationship: more understanding, better communication, more excitement in sex, etc. In short, one partner wants to grow while the other is "satisfied" or sees no need to change. Well, from VIM's point of view it takes two people working together to get the most out of the partnership. A surprising thing usually happens. The reluctant partner will eventually agree to "cooperate" only to find that as the process develops they become eagerly enthusiastic. Perhaps this should not be too surprising after all. There is the potential of a tremendous personal satisfaction and excitement in opening up authentic intimacy in marriage. The best possible solution would be an attitude of both partners which would go something like this:

> "Part of my personal growth and personal happiness depends upon my relationship with you. Therefore, I want to take every opportunity to explore this partnership so that I

can continually discover the enriching experience of the intimate potential that we can share."

This may not be quite your style of saying things. You may want to work on your communication with each other or your "sex life" together. The point is to agree to experience VIM together if for no other reasons than to share an adventure with each other.

It is only fair that you know a little about what you will be getting into. Basically, in VIM we deal with positive, effective verbal and touch communication between married partners. This total process is the evolution of intimacy.

One of the main problems with the term *intimacy* is the strong association with "sexual intimacy." For an alarming number of couples, *intimacy* is foreplay and intercourse. It is no wonder then that millions of partners have asked the sad question:

"Isn't there more to marriage than this?"

It is not unusual for many of these same couples to start collecting a variety of "how to" sex books and to try a hundred variations on the same theme only to discover that intimacy is part creativity—like making love hanging from a chandelier—and part something else. It is the "something else" that we want to give a chance to develop through VIM. It has been our experience that couples who can really get in touch with the "something else" are the ones who vitalize intimacy in marriage. Hopefully, by putting intimacy into a different perspective, VIM will enable your relationship to take on exciting new dimensions.

Nowhere in this book do we talk about extramarital sex, swinging, swapping, or bringing in a third party to spice up your marriage. We also will not go into problems of religion, in-laws, contraception, child rearing, or finances. This book is written for you, the marital pair, as an informative, experiential venture into expanding intimate communication. We hope that it will be an exciting and meaningful way to literally "get in touch" with each other—in more ways than one!

Part I
A Personal Glimpse

Chapter 1

Before We Say, "I Do"

We met, we laughed, we played, we talked, we worked, we shared, we cared, and then we loved. We talked of marriage, and then we were afraid.

Each of us had been married before (Robert, 15 years, Patricia, 12 years) and both our marriages had ended in divorce. Each of us could still remember our own wedding day and all the thoughts and feelings that led to our decision to marry—feelings of love, caring, and sharing, and thoughts that we were different somehow than all the other lovers in the world.

Here we were now, Robert and Patricia, many many years later talking about marriage to each other—we had a right to be afraid.

Our main concern at this point was not to hypothesize about why our earlier marriages ended in divorce nor to insure that our marriage to each other stand the test of time, i.e., not end in divorce, but rather to creatively pursue the process of vitalizing intimacy in our marriage. What could we do to keep our relationship moving in a positive direction? Our relationship was warm, exciting, meaningful, and packed full of caring and understanding; we knew that becoming husband and wife was not the destination but only the vehicle through which our relationship could grow.

Independently of each other, we set out to do a little "soul searching"—an exploration into the attitudes and behaviors which we believed essential to this process.

We attended numerous workshops and seminars related to marital and sexual problems, we read extensively in the area of marriage, and we reflected on our previous marital experiences.

All of these efforts seemed to be more frustrating than beneficial as far as our exploration was concerned. The workshops and seminars concentrated primarily on problem resolution with some emphasis on problem prevention. The books on marriage tended to relate the history of marriage; its function in society; its problem areas, "critical periods," concerns of child rearing, contraception, and positions for intercourse. Our reflections on our previous marital experiences again seemed to be problem-prevention oriented and therefore not that appropriate to the task which we had set for ourselves.

We were not denying the realities of problems in marriage nor were we overlooking the need to be knowledgeable in areas such as child rearing, contraception, and sexual acrobatics. In fact, a lot of thought, discussion, and decision-making went into many of these issues. But our concern was what are the "essentials" involved in vitalizing intimacy in our marriage. Not how to keep from "upsetting the apple cart," but rather, how to make the cart overflow with delicious fruits!

We finally found our "essentials" through reflecting on *our relationship with each other.* We attempted to delineate the dynamics of our own relationship. Each of us began to make a list of attitudes and behaviors we appreciated in ourselves and in each other. These lists, written on newsprint, also contained those attitudes and behaviors that we had not necessarily experienced with each other but which we believed to be an integral component of vitalizing intimacy.

We brought our newsprint together one evening, hung them on the walls, and sat in the middle of the floor quite disconcerted. We had both been rather wordy in our lists—the entire walls of the room were covered. It seemed almost an impossible task to integrate and consolidate them into a meaningful whole. We began to share our ideas with each other. We discussed and clarified issues—we discovered a lot about ourselves, each other, and our relationship.

We spent many evenings in this way and ultimately agreed upon five areas which we felt were representative of the various "specifics" we had listed.

1. Who Are You?

Because we are evolving persons and partners, we realize it is illogical to assume or take each other for granted. Therefore, we will actively seek to discover the "newness" in each other. Marriage offers us the opportunity of discovering our familiar partner in a new and different way.

2. There Are Three of Us.

We are two separate and distinct individuals who have created a third unique entity—our relationship. We will protect, nurture, and facilitate the growth of each of these three entities.

3. Where Are We Going?

Marriage is no more or no less than what we make it. We will give it top priority. We will devote time, energy, effort, and thought into making it a creative partnership.

4. Let's Touch Each Other.

Physical intimacy is more than sex. It includes many, many behaviors—holding hands, a kiss, intercourse, a face caress, etc., each of which is meaningful in and of itself. We will explore these behaviors freely, openly, and spontaneously as a means of intensifying and celebrating our relationship.

5. Let's Talk with Each Other about Ourselves.

Communication which represents the self is necessary for personal and interpersonal growth. It is necessary to create the relationship. Therefore, we will share our thoughts and feelings as clearly and as unambiguously as we can.

These areas are further developed and expanded throughout this book. You must keep in mind that these "essentials" were developed by us, for us. In this sense they are unique to our own personal relationship, thus, they *can not* be considered *the* guidelines to vitalizing intimacy in every marriage! We are acutely aware of the differing desires, goals, and expectations that each partner and each couple has for its own marriage. We recognize that the responsibility lies within each couple as to the guidelines it will set for itself. We definitely feel that VIM can help in this endeavor. It will help you focus on your own unique relationship and, hopefully, create your own special intimacy.

Chapter 2
Marital Health

Our personal interest in vitalizing intimacy in our own marriage played a significant role in crystallizing our professional efforts in the area of Marital Health. We saw the need for "something" to act as a catalyst in facilitating the intimacy that partners can share in marriage. We began working on developing a program to assist couples in this regard. We were interested in the marital *health* of the couple. We wanted to emphasize problem prevention, personal and relationship enrichment, and the positive aspects of marriage rather than the more traditional crisis-intervention approach. For the most part, couples tend to wait until a real crisis occurs in their marriage and then come to a therapist for assistance.

On the other hand, a vision of Marital Health is to:

—Develop a preventative approach to marital therapy by encouraging marital health checkups similar to physical and dental checkups. This approach would also include marriage-enrichment experiences to meet the increasing number of partners who want to take every opportunity of constructively exploring the dimensions of their unique partnership.

—Conduct quality research on how and why marriages

became successful. Volumes have been written on the pathology of marriage and why they fail. There is a great need to discover the characteristics of healthy marriages.

—Establish a National Marital Health Week which would call attention to the marital pair as the basic nucleus of our society. We already honor our parental roles with Mother's Day and Father's Day.

—Provide educational and training workshops for professionals and married couples interested in promoting and putting into practice the concepts of Marital Health.

It is really amazing when you stop to think about it. Here we are in the twentieth century. A time of social progress and change. We have innovative programs in family planning, maternal care, and child care. Issues on abortion, civil rights, sexual liberation, the right to live, and the right to die are being faced for the first time. Emphasis has been placed on health specialty fields such as mental health, dental health, school health, environmental health, and child health.

Yet with all of these innovative ideas we have still neglected a striving majority of citizens who make up the backbone of the American culture. This is not the American family as is so often thought. The family has received a tremendous amount of funds, support, research, and educational programs from local, federal, and state agencies. Rightly so, we are concerned with sex education, juvenile delinquency, drug addiction, and many other family-related problems. But what about the quality of life of those two especially important people that form the nucleus of the American family? What has been done to focus on the marital partnership as a source for wholesome family growth and development? Most married couples want their relationship to be a constant and growing source of personal and interpersonal joy, meaningfulness, and satisfaction. Few can see clearly how to accomplish this but many desperately want it to happen in their own marriage.

The demands of our society are great. Married couples give continually to civic, church, school, family, and professional demands. The individual talents, efforts, and time of married partners is being expended more and more outside the marriage. Surely we must known by now that marriage requires time and personal attention if it is to meet our expectation for intimacy.

This is the mission of marital health and if it is to become a reality it needs the support of every American citizen—single, married, and divorced. The quality of every marriage, in one way or another, affects all. Perhaps the time is near when *Marital Health* will be not only a household phrase but a dynamic process within every household.

Chapter 3
Pairing Enrichment Program (PEP)

As co-directors of Marital Health Studies in the department of psychiatry, we are involved in both marital therapy and sex therapy. However several years ago we became aware of a growing number of couples who did not need a crisis-intervention approach but wanted to learn more about effective social and intimate communication skills for promoting their own marital growth and development. Based upon our personal and professional experience, we developed the Pairing Enrichment Program, or PEP, to help meet this need. We selected this name because it implies the focus is on the *pair*—the marital dyad—husband and wife. We did not intend to de-emphasize "the family," however it was definitely our intention to emphasize the "marital pair."

PEP is a couple-oriented, educational, experiential program designed to discover and explore the intimate potential of effective communication in marriage. The three-week program is initially a weekend experience. At the end of the weekend experience, each couple is given a three-week follow-up booklet which is followed at home. At the end of this period, we see each couple for a follow-up session. We also see them again privately three months and one year following the PEP weekend. We call these three-month and one-year follow-ups "marital health checkups" and take these opportunities to evaluate the effectiveness of the program and to gather important information on how they are keeping their marriage moving, in a positive, meaningful direction. We have found that by this time we can learn a great deal from the PEP couples. In effect, PEP has evolved over the years largely through the feedback of several hundred couples who have participated in the experience. PEP has proved to be one of the most rewarding experiences we have ever personally and professionally undertaken. Our faith in marital health and the process of marriage enrichment is continually renewed by each PEP experience and by the many couples who are celebrating the warmth of their own marriages.

Both PEP and VIM are based on the five "essentials" which we shared with you briefly in chapter 1. We really had no way of knowing whether or not these ingredients of vitalizing intimacy in marriage would be applicable to a general population. They have only become strengthened with time. We have been encouraged by many PEP participants to write a book based on these guidelines and the PEP experience. Of course there is no way we can put PEP into book form but perhaps we can share with you some of our ideas of marriage enrichment and expanding intimacy in marriage. Perhaps our experience can help to identify the variety of attitudes about marriage and intimacy that tend to block effective communication in marriage. Perhaps we can suggest some ways to overcome these blocks to vitalizing intimacy in marriage. This then is the purpose of VIM. We have designed the book as a positive adventure in marriage. However, VIM as PEP is only a beginning. Indeed every day in a marriage relationship is a beginning. We make of it what we choose to for intimacy in marriage is created. There is no time to do anything less and there is absolutely no better time to start than now, so let's begin.

Part II
Delusions About Marriage - The DAM's

Chapter 4

Marriage Is What You Think It Is

Most married partners have some ideas on what marriage *should* be like. There is probably a fairly good consensus on what a marriage should provide in terms of personal growth, satisfaction, and happiness. Most couples would like to find the marriage a fun and exciting relationship. Perhaps full of those special moments that acknowledge each partner as a very special person. Marriage is the place where personal ideas, interests, and feelings can be shared with someone who cares and understands. It is a relationship where two people experience a unique meaningfulness for each other. It is a source for self-worth and self-esteem. Marriage is the one place both partners can really be themselves. Communication is free and open and full of surprises as both partners learn more about themselves and each other. Marriage is feeling that special closeness, intimacy, and emotional pleasure with each other. Marriage is a celebration, a recreation, a way of saying thank-you.

A lot of this may sound somewhat idealistic and rather abstract. This is probably because in reality most American marriages never rise much above the level of mediocracy or complacency. This is certainly not because married partners do not want to fulfill the potential of their partnership or do not want their marriage to approach an ideal. The problem is that couples have very little opportunity to learn how to relate effectively with each other. Most learning of this sort is by trial-and-error and often the errors predominate.

In addition to the lack of training directed toward more productive communication in marriages, there are some *attitudes* that apparently work against the idea of creativity in marriage. We will refer to these attitudinal blocks as *Delusions About Marriage* or *DAM's*. There are many DAM's and most of us believe in some of them in one form or another. From our experience in counseling we know that these DAM's can exert a powerfully destructive influence on the marriage relationship. We also know that many marriages can take on a new and more fulfilling dimension once these DAM's are recognized and broken. It is as if that trapped potential that is behind every DAM is suddenly released and partners finally begin to really communicate and share intimately with each other. Breaking through DAM's can be difficult but not impossible. The first step is recognizing that a particular DAM is indeed operating in your marriage. The next step would be to determine how this DAM is restraining or preventing the process of intimacy for you and your partner. The final step is doing something about it and then experiencing the resulting change in the relationship.

Some of the DAM's are often built because they were actually started from early childhood. Our attitudes about marriage are shaped by many sources including parents, relatives, friends, and the sociocultural environment in which we were reared. However, even a small crack in a DAM can result in tremendous changes within the marriage partnership. For example, one of the DAM's that most American couples start building on the wedding day is that marriage will take care of itself without any special effort. On the other hand, the philosophy of VIM is that *doing* something about your marriage on a day-to-day, moment-by-moment basis is one of the most important endeavors you can ever undertake. Why? Because by being good at being married, you have that very special opportunity of discovering *your own* potential for growth *through* the experience of your relatedness in marriage. This is not something to take lightly. It is not an "optional extra" of marriage. It is rather the mainspring of *Vitalizing Intimacy in Marriage.*

Marriage is the process of two people evolving as persons through the partnership. The process never ends, but it also never gets started unless each partner takes the initiative to do something constructive about the marriage. In short, marriage is what you think it is. Let's look at some of the common delusions about marriage—and see if you can begin to think about them differently.

Chapter 5

DAM One: Marriage Will Just Naturally Take Care of Itself

This delusion about marriage has been referred to as the "myth of naturalism" which implies that once married you just *naturally* know how to live happily ever after. In one sense, marriage is natural. Often people marry without really thinking about what marriage is or what they expect it to be, or more importantly, what they want to make it. It is just one of those things that people do at a certain age or time or when they experience a certain feeling.

The reasons for creating a relationship with another person vary widely. The decision to marry or the *natural* evolvement into marriage also varies. But from counseling with married partners we have learned one thing about marriage that seems to remain constant. That is the belief in DAM 1—marriage will just naturally take care of itself. In other words, married partners do not have to work on their relationship because marriage is a natural process. Many couples actually feel *guilty* when they find they have to work on their relationship. It is as if they perceive working on their marriage as meaning that they are not "successful" or that they do not "naturally" love each other. They began to question their feelings (their love) for each other rather than facing the real question of their behaviors.

Partners tend to think and behave as if marriage is a condition which requires no time, no energy, no sharing, no creativity, and yet, expect it to provide meaning, warmth, joy, excitement, and undying love. However, these same partners expend a lot of time, energy, and emotional input in meeting vocational responsibilities, hobby, and recreational needs, children's needs, social needs, civic needs, church needs, and any number of other needs and responsibilities. If there is any time or energy left for the marriage relationship, it may well be at ten o'clock at night, in bed, dead tired, with each partner wondering if the other really wants sex tonight.

There are some built-in responsibilities in marriage. Occasionally partners have to take time out from their busy schedules to be with each other. At these times the communication is typically problem-oriented. The sharing of thoughts and feelings usually evolve around the maintenance needs of the family: finances, children, work, in-laws, and social obligations. What about the marital dyad—me, you? What about the relationship—us? Suggestion:

> Think back for a moment on your own progression into marriage. When, how, and where did you meet? What pleased you most about yourself at that time? About your partner? Why did you select this person to be your spouse? What did you expect your marriage to be like? What made your relationship special?

Probably the relationship you shared was in focus. No doubt you took special notice of each other. The chances are you openly communicated with each other and listened to each other because you wanted to learn about yourself, your partner, and your relationship.

We are not suggesting that you recapture these early days, but if you find it obvious that your marriage has slipped from top priority to last priority, we do suggest acknowledging the following:

> A marriage relationship needs creativity from both partners if it is to become more than just a home management seminar. It must be put into focus. It needs tending to. If you are waiting for intimacy to occur "naturally" then you will most naturally be disappointed.

The Relationship Business

We are indebted to a couple who came to us for counseling a couple of years ago because they inadvertently provided us with some insight and a label for a concept we had felt for some time and had been struggling with articulating. We will refer to them as Mr. and Mrs. Business because they tended to think of everything in terms of productions, responsibilities, management, assets, and liabilities. They owned and operated three very successful businesses. They prided themselves on their abilities to do so, particularly because they had had no special training—"We did it on our own. It takes a lot of work, but it is worth it." Their marriage was the only unsuccessful business that they had undertaken. In terms of years, it too was successful. They had been married twelve years. In terms of money, children, house, and luxuries they were exceedingly successful. They prided themselves on this as well and attributed the success of their marriage to their running it like a business. Each had his or her own responsibilities, and production was great. Saturday was his day to make house and auto repairs, take care of the lawn, and review their personal finances. It was her day to wash clothes, clean the house, and do the grocery shopping.

Why had they come to us for counseling? "Something is missing. I do not know really how to describe it because I am not sure what it is. It is not something you can really put your finger on. I even feel silly talking about it, but it is a feeling—really it is a lack of feeling. I guess I do not feel like a "special" person in our marriage. Somehow things have changed between us. There is no 'spark' anymore."

We explored their relationship further. Every attempt we made to offer suggestions to enrich their relationship was interrupted by one of them explaining again and again to us that they did not have time for that because they had three businesses to run as well as the marriage business which was no easy task. It was at this point that the insight and label of "The Relationship Business" was finally articulated.

We suggested to them that twelve years ago they had become partners in the business of marriage. They had been successful in that business. But what about their *relationship* with each other? Was that not also a "business"? Isn't the *relationship* between man and woman separate from the business of marriage?

We suggested to them that their twelve-year partnership with each other could become the most intimate and rewarding business that they could ever have if they would treat their relationship as a business. It had never occurred to either of them that the relationship between the two of them was a special kind of business—*a relationship business*. Put in this light, it made all the difference in the world. This couple could understand their relationship in terms of a business because they realized that any business requires time, energy, creative input, and work if it is to be successful. Unfortunately, it is not unusual for partners to put more creativity, thought, and time each week into "outside" interests than they give to their relationship on a yearly basis. The Incidental Marriage is usually the result.

The Incidental Marriage

John and Mary had been married 15 years. Early in their marriage they would spend a great deal of time alone just talking, touching, and feeling good together. They would take long silent walks together, hand-in-hand, feeling the warmth of each other's presence. These times were important and very special for both of them. They would often change their plans or adjust their schedules in order to *make* time to be together. After a few years they had their first child, and two more children soon followed. John was admired by his employer and business associates for his ingenuity and creativity, and it was not long before he advanced into an executive position. This required extra hours of hard work away from home. His work became a great source of pleasure for him. He also enjoyed golf and most weekends found him on the course "unwinding."

During John's rapid rise to success, Mary spent most of her time with the children. After eight years of marriage, Mary decided to become active in civic work. At first, this was just a welcome diversion from the chores at home, but she became more and more involved and eventually was elected an officer in several organizations and clubs. Not only was Mary well liked but she was greatly appreciated for her leadership and organizational abilities.

John and Mary have evolved into what we call the *Incidental Marriage*. In other words their marriage had become an incidental feature in their lives. Sure, they would occasionally get together in the same house on the same night for sex or to have a meal together but this was just about the extent of their "marriage." They became more and more critical of each other because the marriage often became a source of inconvenience to their other interests.

John and Mary's Incidental Marriage continued for several years. It may have lasted longer if it was not for John's heart attack. It was a mild attack but it did slow him down long enough for him to think about what he was doing and where he was going. The long and frequent visits to the hospital also slowed Mary down enough to allow her time to think about what was happening. When John came home, they talked. They talked all night and over breakfast the next day. They suddenly realized that they had not eaten breakfast together in years. They also discovered to their utter amazement that the longest single period of time that they had been together, really together, in the last ten years was when Mary visited John in the hospital. For the first time in ten years, they *communicated* with each other about their relationship. They discovered a lot about each other. More importantly they found they really wanted to learn more about each other. They wanted to renew their *relationship*.

There are literally hundreds of different kinds of Incidental Marriages. The details may change but the plot is the same. It is an attitude: I do this and that, I am this and that, I play this and that, I want to be this and that—and—*incidentally*, I am married. It is our guess that the majority of American marriages accept the DAM that marriage will just "naturally" take care of itself. Believing in this DAM invariably places the relationship at the bottom of the list as far as time, effort, creativity, and involvement are concerned. Most of us firmly believe that if we want to succeed in our profession, in our hobbies, or any other endeavor, we have to work on it. The relationship between married partners is no different.

We think the day is finally coming where society says it is O.K. to work on your marriage. Working on your relationship no longer means you are on the brink of divorce or that you no longer love each other. It means your relationship is important and meaningful and you want to give it top priority. You want to make it the most it can be for you and for your partner. Love alone does not make it happen. It is your love for each other that motivates each of you to take full responsibility for making it happen. If you are looking for more than adjustment and compatibility in your marriage, if you are not willing to settle for an Incidental Marriage or to be housemates who share only the responsibilities and burdens of marriage, then each partner must assume responsibility to do something about it—it won't happen naturally!

Relationship Contact Points

Relationship Contact Points are those creative and independent events which focus on the here-and-now process of the marriage relationship. In John and Mary's case they discovered that they indeed had created no special relationship contact points in the last ten years of their marriage. Their house, which once was their own private "love nest" had become nothing more than a convenient place to eat and sleep. The management of it had in fact become a burden. If they did go out together, it was always with business associates or with a group of friends. On the few occasions in which they found themselves alone at home together, they frantically thought of things to do or people to invite over to occupy their time. Any communication between them was invariably about their outside interest, the children's behavior or school work, what needed to be done around the house, or who had the time to take Johnny to the dentist. Sex was about the only "contact point" they had and that was mostly conducted out of need rather than experienced out of pleasure.

John's illness resulted in a very meaningful transition in their marriage. It had brought their relationship into focus. By their focusing outside the marriage, they had effectively avoided the very real risk involved in focusing in. It was awkward at first—they felt like strangers. The first step for them was to create a special type of relationship contact point—a once-a-week "business meeting." This was a time set aside just for them to be alone with each other. There was no agenda or topics that had to be discussed. Rather this was an opportunity to explore the dimensions of the relationship—an opportunity to share their personal needs; an opportunity to express feelings about themselves, each other, and their unique partnership; an opportunity to get acquainted with this special "stranger." Business meetings were not a time to discuss finances, politics, children, the house, in-laws or for chitchat. They were simply times to experience the presence of the relationship.

These "business meetings" continued and other relationship contact points were incorporated into their busy schedules. They continued to have children, family, and social obligations. John still worked long hours and Mary continued to serve as an officer in several organizations. These responsibilities had not been the primary cause of their estrangement, but rather their failure to consciously *create* their relationship. Rather than trying to "make the world go away," they made time for the two of them in that world. They turned some of the household chores into relationship contact points. Making beds and lining shelves became opportunities for them to communicate and play with each other.

They took the responsibility for *creating* other relationship contact points. They made dinner "dates" with each other—sometimes to go to a restaurant and other times for a candlelight meal at home together. One relationship contact point they found especially meaningful to them was bathing each other. They had showered together before when they were in a hurry to get some place. This time rather than fighting over the soap or struggling to get under the flow of water, they bathed each other. Very gently without a word, each bathed and was bathed from head to toe—even the hidden places. They felt warm and close and cared for and very special.

John and Mary were beginning to get in touch with that most important asset of marriage—the relationship. It was an exciting and new adventure for them because, for the first time in their married lives, they had taken a step to vitalize intimacy in their relationship rather than letting the marriage just *naturally* take care of itself.

Concepts

In this chapter we have introduced two concepts which can help to break the DAM that marriage will just naturally take care of itself.

1. The Marriage Relationship Business Meeting. This is a special time set aside on a once-a-week or twice-a-month basis for married partners to literally "get in touch" with the unique relationship they share. The meeting can last from a few minutes to several hours. It is not the time or place for the meetings that is important. What is important is putting your relationship in focus and giving it no less than it deserves.

   The purpose of this meeting is to:

   A. Focus on each partner's feelings, needs, pleasures, and problems with *self*, with *partner*, and with *relationship*.

   B. Be able to share this important information with each other without accusing, demanding, or counseling. Sharing information in the form of ideas, attitudes, and feelings will become a negative and unproductive experience only if *either partner* allows that to happen. The business meeting is not a gripe session—it is an exploration into *all* of the dimensions of the relationship. The business meeting offers each partner an opportunity to gain some insight and understanding of the process of a creative marriage relationship. This means that each partner has the responsibility of maintaining a constructive dialogue. Only by helping each other to communicate effectively can issues be discussed, needs be expressed, and goals be established.

C. Allow periodic evaluation of the progress in developing a positive movement of the relationship in the direction of greater personal and interpersonal satisfaction and meaning.

2. Relationship Contact Points (RCP's). This concept is concerned with the moment-by-moment interaction of married partners. It originated several years ago when we realized the need to develop a mechanism to help couples break away from some of the rigid domestic roles that we take as "givens" from our culture. For example, it is a woman's job to clean house, make up the beds, and prepare the meals. It is a man's job to mow the grass, fix leaky faucets, and take out the garbage. For the most part, these activities become chores which have little reward value.

On the other hand, these activities as well as many others can be accomplished in an entirely different way by both partners. Rather than emphasizing the "job" that has to be assigned and done many couples use this time as RCP's. The relationship is emphasized. By working together this can be a time for communication, playing together, touching each other, etc. Most couples who have turned household "chores" into RCP's have discovered some quite rewarding changes in both attitudes and behaviors.

We were recently discussing the concept of RCP's before a group when a woman said, "I just don't see how helping to fix a tractor can be a fun experience." The point is well taken. We are certainly not suggesting that everything that has to be done must be done together. However, there are many "chores" that can be fun to do together. From our experience many of these same "chores" are areas of conflict between partners who have operated under the rigid role assigning system.

Turning chores into RCP's is only one practical behavioral application of this concept. The real intent of RCP's, however, is to take advantage of all opportunities to relate with each other in the present.

Chapter 6

DAM Two: Boredom Is a Natural Consequence of Marriage

Mr. and Mrs. Nothingsnew came to us for counseling. We met them in the waiting room, led them back to our counseling office and observed them as they positioned themselves as far apart from each other as possible on the sofa in front of us. We had already read the forms they had completed which asked for some background data and why they were seeking counseling. From these forms, we knew he was 29, she was 25. They had been married three years, no children. Both were college graduates. Both were bored.

We asked if they would like a cup of coffee. Both said yes, and the husband added that he would like cream in his coffee. The wife almost jumped off the sofa. She looked at us as if she were in a state of shock and said, "No, he doesn't. He drinks his coffee black!" Did he do that to shock her or had he been drinking his coffee with cream for the last two years and she simply had not noticed?

As we drank our coffee, the following emerged:

Mrs. Nothingsnew:

"We've been married three years, need I say more? He gets up at 6:30, goes to work, comes home, eats dinner, watches t.v., and goes to bed."

Mr. Nothingsnew:

"Well we've done all there is to do, we've said all there is to say. We know everything there is to know about each other. What more do you expect? There is *nothing new*." (Hence, their name: Nothingsnew.)

There was silence. It seemed endless, and then Mr. Nothingsnew continued:

"Well, it's the strangest thing. We dated two years before we married and during that time I'll have to admit there was never a dull moment. It seemed like we were always into something—like one night at 11:00 we decided it would be fun to pack up and go to the beach. Well, within one hour we were in the car and on our way! We think of things like that now, but never follow through. Somehow we don't feel as free as we used to."

Mrs. Nothingsnew:

"He's absolutely right. We used to do those crazy fun things. At first, we were just sort of having fun playing house. We used to make a game out of making up the bed together, washing the dishes, figuring out our budget. We even made a game out of a chore we both hated—washing windows. He would be on the outside and I was on the inside. We would make faces at each other and laugh so hard we could hardly clean the window. But like I said, that was some time ago before we began to take marriage so seriously I guess. Now we've each got our own duties and responsibilities.

And another thing that I really don't understand is how we can think so differently about things. For example, we used to meet after work at this place where a lot of our friends met to play backgammon. We might play until seven or eight and then go home and cook dinner. Well, now I feel like I *must* go right home after work and cook and I'm angry with him if he stops by for a game!"

Mr. Nothingsnew:

"You know, we both want our marriage to be a good one. I guess we're in a dilemma: we want the fun and spontaneity we had and yet, don't we have to settle down? Are all good marriages boring?"

Mr. and Mrs. Nothingsnew had come to believe what they had heard so often—when you get married you have to "settle down" because marriage is "serious business." They had interpreted this to mean you need to become rigid, role-assigning, and routine.

After only three years of marriage they had worked all of the uncertainty and spontaniety out of their relationship and had settled down to the seriousness of marriage. Mr. and Mrs. Nothingsnew represent many couples who have lived together for any length of time. However, this does not mean that marriage inherently leads to the Nothingsnew Syndrome. Marriage is no more than what the two individuals *make* it on a day-to-day basis. This couple had blocked any possibility for newness and discovery by their self-defeating assumption: Boredom is a natural consequence of marriage.

We are frankly getting a little tired of books on marriage and sex that imply that boredom and routine replaces excitement and discovery in relationships of any duration. There is probably nothing more devastating to the idea of continually creating a dynamic marriage than the "settling down" myth that so many couples seem to follow. Quite frequently, we hear couples say:

> "Well, of course, the newness and those feelings of excitement about the relationship has worn a little thin over the past few years. I guess that's to be expected, isn't it?"

Let's compare this attitude with another that was expressed to us recently:

> "I've been married seventeen years and have two teenage daughters. I feel a little silly saying this because I guess it's not your typical reaction but I still get that excited jittery feeling every time my husband comes home from work. I really don't know what the difference is but I can truly say that our marriage is far from being dull. My friends have told me that we have an unusual marriage. I suppose it's because we are involved in each other."

When the Nothingsnew DAM infiltrates the mind, it blinds the eyes and deafens the ears. In this state, one loses sight and sound of the unique person and partner whose very being is unfolding before them. There is no chance for growth without change and not acknowledging and recognizing that change either in ourselves or in our partner is to restrict or cancel out any potential for developing a dynamic relationship.

The Changing Aspect of the Present Relationship

There is absolutely no way anyone can know on a moment-to-moment basis what their partner is feeling or thinking because we are changing people. We are not the same person or partner we were twenty years ago or even yesterday. We are evolving persons. Because we are changing persons *and* partners, our relationship necessarily is changing. A *dynamic* relationship means that we are in the process of discovering ourselves and our partner anew. In other words, we are experiencing a "familiar" partner differently.

This concept of change is so important. Most people would agree that it is true, yet so few *behave* as if it were. Apparently one of the hardest things for many partners to acknowledge is the fact that their spouse has really changed after all. Quite often in our counseling sessions one partner will interrupt the other with, "But that hasn't happened in years! I have changed so much. Why can't you see me the way I am now!"

Quite often the past will not let partners change in their spouses' eyes. The Nothingsnew Marriage gets that way because partners indeed *think* that there is nothing new. Little do they know and how much they could learn if they would communicate (and that includes listening) effectively. Keeping in touch with the *changing aspects of the present relationship* is an important process of marriage.

The wife who expressed feelings of excitement and anticipation on hearing her husband's car pull into the driveway after seventeen years of marriage had discovered *this* very important process. Her attitude (and that of her husband) made this process work for their relationship. Each day offered her the opportunity to fully explore the newness in her familiar partner. Indeed, she was *involved*. She was involved in discovering herself and her partner through the totality of their relationship. Such discovery does not happen by chance. It is a product of sharing information about the person we are becoming in the relationship. There are some good ways to begin to put this into practice.

I-Messages

One way that is so effective in giving each other information and letting each other know who we are on a moment-by-moment basis is by using I-messages.

I-messages are one of the most powerful tools we know in developing a dynamic marriage relationship. In the first place, it encourages *self-representation* in the marriage. Partners who represent themselves in their communication and try not to represent their partner are opening the way to discovery. Unfortunately, some married partners tend to talk *to* each other as if they know what is best for the other. Or they talk *for* their partner as they assume or second guess what their spouse feels, thinks, and does. Obviously communicating *to* or *for* your partner offers nothing to keeping communication open and discovering anything new about each other.

During counseling sessions, we often hear couples talking to or for each other. The result is usually a growing distance between them as they assume more and more responsibility for each other's communication. The kind of language that is used in this situation is often you-messages rather than I-messages. For example:

You never . . .
You always . . .
You should . . .
You ought to . . .
You are . . .
You can't . . .
You can . . .

These you-message qualifying statements block communication because they put your partner into adversary court. He or she stands accused and the only recourse is to defend. The problem is that in a marriage by trial proceedings nobody wins.

There is another form of you-message that occurs quite

often. This form is sometimes used because we are genuinely concerned about what our partner would like. That is, we may have good intentions but the results can be devastating. For example:

"What would you like to do?"
"I don't know, what would you like to do?"
"Well suggest something."
"Would you like to go to a show?"
"It's alright with me if you want to."
"Well, we ought to do something. I thought you liked to go to the movies."
Etc., etc., etc.

This is a case where the you-message puts the responsibility on your partner. If you finally end up going to a movie and you did not enjoy it you can always blame your partner for not suggesting something better to do.

With I-messages you learn to communicate *with* each other rather than *to* or *for* each other. You can give each other very valuable information about self-in-relationship. In other words with I-messages you become a part of the partnership. I-messages are characterized by sentences which began with "I". For example:

I feel . . .
I am afraid . . .
I would like . . .
I want to . . .
I think that . . .
I find that . . .

One of the best I-messages of all is the simple "I love you." With this statement you have taken ownership of your own feelings. You have represented yourself in communicating that feeling, and you have expressed that feeling with the security that it will be accepted. All of this is the process of developing I-message skills.

I-messages are often difficult to do in many marriage relationships but couples who have practiced this important way to relate *with* each other have found it to be a tremendous help in keeping communication and discovery open.

Chapter 12

DIM Two: Sex Is Something You Do TO or FOR Your Partner

If you think sex is something you do *to* your partner it's unfortunate but understandable. Why? Because as we said earlier sexual attitudes are learned, and what we learned about sex is largely dependent on whether we were born male or female. Being born male, of course, implies that as an adult you know everything there is to know about sex (even if you have been too afraid to ask) and it also implies you are a sexual being whose sexual needs must be met. Being born female, on the other hand, implies you do not know anything about sex and further more you do not care to know anything because you are not a sexual being. You have no sexual interest and certainly no sexual feelings. This sad state of affairs was perpetuated by male authors being the sole contributors to our vast "knowledge" of sex education. The whole area of sex was the male's domain. The male was the sexual expert who was endowed with divine sexual knowledge. He, after all, had sexual experience and feelings that he acquired from nobody in particular and everybody in general. This probably accounts for the overabundance of myths and misconceptions about female sexuality. The myth that females had no sexual feelings led quite logically to the belief that *sex is something the husband does to his wife.*

Husband's attitude:

> It is a wife's duty to give her husband sex whenever he wants it. I have made it clear that if I do not get it at home, I will sure find it somewhere else. I hate to put it that way but that is just the way it is.

During this sex-to era, females were naive, chaste, pure, and unaffected with sexual desire. To be anything less was to be classified as a loose woman who obviously no self-respecting male would want to marry or for that matter be with any longer than necessary. When she did marry, she was an enduring receptacle for her husband's penis. Any sexual feelings she had were usually repressed.

Wife's Attitude:

> I know (my mother told me) that it is a wife's duty to satisfy her husband. Sex is important to him so I try never to refuse him. I want to keep him satisfied at home.

If you think sex is something you do *for* your partner it is again unfortunate, but also understandable. Why? Because in the 1940s with the help of the Kinsey studies, we learned that females do have sexual interests and feelings and can even be orgasmic! On the surface this seems like a liberating bit of knowledge. No longer did the dutiful wife have to conceal her sexual feelings. It would seem that now since both husband and wife could admit they were sexual beings, they could really begin to enjoy sharing fully their sexuality with each other. But, this was naive because the myth that man was the sexual expert still existed. Man's enviable status carried with it a burdening responsibility: he had to do *for* his wife. After all, she was capable of sexual pleasure (even orgasms) and he alone knew what, how and when to give her pleasure. It was no longer the wife's responsibility to give her husband pleasure, but his instead, to give her pleasure.

Wife's attitude:

> Frankly, I resent him not giving me an orgasm. He doesn't know how to turn me on. He tries so hard that sometimes I just fake it because I know he will feel bad if I don't.

Husband's attitude:

> We used to have sex a lot but now it has turned into work for me. It takes me so long to get her ready. You know what I mean?

Attitudes of doing *to* and *for* your partner are at last being replaced by the *sharing with* attitude. If you think sex is something you share *with* your partner then you realize that males and females are sexual equals, that is, each partner is equally responsible for his or her *own* feelings. Rather than assigning responsibility to one sex or the other, we are now entering into an era where married partners can begin to freely explore and create a *shared* intimacy with each other. This transition of to-for, and with has resulted largely from the significant studies of Masters and Johnson. We now know that the male is not *the* sex expert (neither is the female) but rather *each* partner is the world's authority on his/her own sexual desires and feelings.

Interplay

For both husbands and wives the responsibility for sexual behaviors and feelings rest with each partner. With this attitude *both* partners are free to explore and feel *with* each other. Rather than becoming a task or a goal, sex becomes an *exchange* in which both partners can attend to their own feelings *and* their partners. It is this intense and *equal sharing* that can create so much personal pleasure and interpersonal meaning to the sexual experience. The thing that is so unique about this equal sharing of responsibility *with* each other is that it can open up so many new dimensions of intimacy in marriage. The idea of *interplay* replaces the prescriptions and stereotyped sequences of who does what to whom when (push-button sex). It means that *both* partners actively help themselves and their partners to whatever experiences they find enjoyable and pleasurable for both. Sex is an interplay of responding *with* each other on a moment-by-moment basis.

Sometimes it may be fun to "do to" or "do for" your partner. This can add variety to the sexual encounter. The point is that if done it should be because both partners are desiring it rather than one partner expecting it. We are all too much aware of the lack of creativity and the number of problems encountered by couples who for years have strictly adhered to the do-to or do-for type of sex. The net result of assigning this type of sexual responsibility to one partner or the other is a loss of sexual identity and freedom of sexual expression which is so important in discovering the pleasures of physical intimacy.

But Isn't It His Responsibility To Give Me an Orgasm?

An orgasm is something that the female *gives herself* permission to have and not something that she "gives" to her husband or her husband "gives" to her. This is a restructured idea from:

> "If I don't have an orgasm he will feel that he is not a good sexual partner—I'd better fake it."
> Or, "I hope I have an orgasm this time because he worked so, hard."

Many husbands still believe that it is their responsibility to "give" their wife an orgasm. This attitude seems to be the most difficult residual of the "do-for" era to leave behind, even though partners agree that the husband's orgasm is simply a *natural* consequence of sex play which has resulted from sexual arousal and activity. The husband may experience a tremendous amount of pleasure in being a part of his wife's orgasm but it hardly is his responsibility to *give* her one.

In the beginning of this section we described the sexual response as a natural physiological function. There is simply no way that we can take over the normal physiological function of our partner. As Masters and Johnson have so adequately put it—we cannot breathe for our partner or eat for our partner or provide an orgasm for our partner. It is each partner's responsibility to:

(1) provide a free expression of one's own needs and desires on a moment-by-moment basis;

(2) to provide an atmosphere of trust and warmth conducive to illiciting a free expression by your partner of his/her needs and desires;

(3) to be as responsive and sensitive to your partner's needs as to your own.

Warning: You must accept *all* three of these responsibilities if you want to create intimacy. Accepting less than all will be more destructive than beneficial. We have found that for most couples it is the first responsibility (freely expressing one's own needs and feelings) that is most frequently ignored. This is not surprising because it seems selfish and most of us were taught that being selfish is bad.

Here is what may happen if you do not communicate your feelings:

Wife:

"Every time we make love I feel like I am literally lying on a bed of eggs! I just don't know what to do. I'm afraid that every move I make will be the wrong one. My husband is a good lover, I guess, but we never talk about what is going on in our sexual relationship. I think that he would be crushed if he really knew how I felt on so many occasions—unsatisfied, confused and even resentful. How many times I thought: "If only he would . . .", or "Why doesn't he stimulate me here now," or "If we could just move into another position," or "I wonder what he would like for me to do now that would give him pleasure?"

Husband:

"Seems like both of us are afraid to express our feelings when it comes to sex. There have been plenty of times that I wished she would just play with me for a while or touch me some place but I never asked. I guess I thought that she would think that I wasn't enjoying myself enough as it was. That's the whole point, we are just playing guessing games with each other."

Sex has been such a secretive topic in our culture that it has been stored away in dark closets, done in dark bedrooms and whispered about in dark corners. No wonder that so many couples are afraid to see it in a better light.

Look at it this way. You are the world's only authority on

what feels good to you and what *you* would like to experience. As the leading authority on this important subject you have the responsibility to let your partner know where you are and what you would like to do on a moment-by-moment basis. There is simply no other way he or she can learn about *you* or know *you* unless *you* communicate. To withhold information from your partner about yourself that could create intimacy is selfish—not the other way around!

If you had an itch on your back you probably would not hesitate to ask your partner to scratch it.

> "I would appreciate your scratching my back, please."
> "Sure, is that the right place?"
> "No, down a little and a little harder too."
> "There?"
> "Not quite, just a little to the right. Now, that's it. That feels so good!"

Why not share the same freedom of communication, giving information in pleasuring each other at a more genital sexual level?

The very best way to communicate in this way is to use what we have described earlier as I-messages. When we are intimately communicating with each other we want to take ownership of our own feelings; to represent ourselves and to give information. I-messages meet these requirements. Remember, I-messages are not meant to be demanding but it is an effective way to communicate.

For example:

> "I would like to feel more pressure here."
> "I would like you to stroke my back."
> "I would like you to turn over now."
> "I would like to move on to something else."
> "I would like to slow down a minute."
> "I would like you to stroke me here about the same way I am doing."
> "I would like to show you what feels good to me."

As you can see, I-messages can be very specific and can yield a lot of information. It is very important that the receiver of I-messages takes this as a valuable opportunity of learning something from his or her partner. This learning experience never ends because we are changing people.

I-Movements

Another aspect of I-messages is what we call I-movements. These are the nonverbal cues that we can give each other. Taking your partner's hand and guiding it to areas you would like to be stimulated or touched is a good example of I-movements. The same would be true in placing your hand over your partner's and showing him or her exactly how much pressure or what rhythm you enjoy feeling on a certain part of your body on this particular occasion. This can often be a very effective learning experience particularly if you are able to move and guide your partner's hand completely.

When two partners are taking a major responsibility for themselves and are communicating effectively—verbally and nonverbally—then there is the potential for growing intimately together. When partners share themselves *with* each other with an open flow of communication and feeling then there is certainly the potential for greater understanding, appreciation, and excitement in their sexual relationship. This involves a special kind of vulnerability—a personal openness and willingness to discover and continually rediscover our self, our partner, and our relationship.

In summary, we suggest that rather than defining the husband's or wife's sexual responsibilities as who does what to whom in order to get someplace, that both partners take equal responsibility in helping themselves and each other toward a more effective sexual sharing. Putting this attitude into practice may involve putting the past aside in favor of a more dynamic discovery of each other in the present and being willing to represent yourself in your relationship *with* your partner.

Chapter 13

DIM Three: Sex Is Having Orgasms

There has been, and still is, a great deal of unnecessary confusion about the female orgasm. Volumes have been written on this subject. Most of which adds to the confusion. Magazine articles flood every household with vivid accounts of women having "real" orgasms. We now have listings of some of the characteristics supposedly influencing a woman's capability of experiencing an orgasm. For example, a woman may be orgasmic if:

1. She was brought up by a father who was dependable, somewhat demanding, but definitely caring.
2. She is married to a man she finds sexually attractive, is a good provider, trustworthy, and encourages self-esteem.
3. She did not grow up with a sexual attitude that was based on shame, guilt, or fear.
4. She is completely satisfied with her birth control device.
5. She has an open, uninhibited approach to sex that includes a free communication with her husband.
6. Her husband is a skilled lover.
7. She masturbates.
8. She knows what the pubococcygeus muscle is and exercises it.
9. She has sexual fantasies.
10. She experiences a sufficient amount of "foreplay."

Ignorance Is Not Bliss

The ability to have an orgasm varies greatly from woman to woman and with the same woman on different occasions. Generally speaking, however, more than just penile thrusting is necessary because the vagina simply does not have that many nerve endings. The clitoris, which has an abundance of nerve endings, is analogous to the male's penis, in that it is the most sexually sensitive part of the woman's body. However, a surprising number of couples are unaware of what the clitoris is, where it is located, or how to stimulate it. How could this be? Well, if you are a woman, your mother or someone probably told you about menstruation and perhaps a little about the birds and bees, but no doubt she didn't tell you that you had a very special organ (the clitoris) which had only one function—*your* pleasure! If you are a man that was probably one of the many things you didn't know about a woman, but were supposed to know and therefore didn't ask. With the advances in sex education, more and more people today are knowledgeable about sex and the sexual apparatus of males and females. Even so, we encounter quite frequently a tendency by many to ignore the facts. Example: Ask any man or woman you know to sketch the male and female pelvic anatomy. No doubt all will include the male's penis. No doubt none will include the female's clitoris! One's ability to sketch or to label accurately the male and female pelvic anatomy is somewhat removed from Vitalizing Intimacy in Marriage. However, when partners in marriage behaviorally ignore "the facts," they cannot expect to create intimacy! Ignorance is not bliss.

Show Me How

The intensity of orgasms varies from woman to woman and with the same woman on different occasions. As far as the physiological intensity of an orgasm is concerned, generally self-stimulation ranks first, manual or oral stimulation by partner second, and intercourse third. (The "subjective" appreciation of an orgasm is probably greater with intercourse.) The best way for any husband to learn how his wife enjoys being erotically stimulated is for him to become a part of the experience. By that we mean he might observe her self-stimulation experience or she could take his hand and fingers and actually guide them in a manner that she finds pleasurable (I-movements). Most husbands would appreciate learning about their wives in this way—assuming of course, that they are open to the discovery.

The same is true the other way around—each man is unique, and different activities are pleasurable at various times. He, too, can show his wife how he likes to be stimulated through self-stimulation or I-movements.

There Is No Substitute

Often partners manually and/or orally stimulate each other at the same time. This is potentially a learning experience for both. It also adds to the variety of ways that partners can share erotically with each other. Frequently, one or both partners will have an orgasm in this way.

A few people hold the attitude that manual or oral stimulation to orgasm by partner is a poor substitute for the Real Thing. Perhaps a more rational approach would be to realize that there is *no substitute for intimacy*. Intimacy is limited only by a couple's lack of creativity and willingness to explore and experience a wide range of shared behaviors.

There is no substitute for kissing, holding hands, or sharing a good meal together. Similarly, there is no substitute for genital pleasure through touching or tasting or thrusting.

The "Real" Orgasm

No doubt you are familiar with the "vaginal" versus "clitoral" orgasm controversy which in effect implies that if you are a mature, i.e., "real" woman you have orgasms through P-in-V intercourse.

Sam and Shirley sat on the sofa across from us in our initial interview with them. They came to us with a "sexual problem." As is typical in our therapy approach, we ask each partner to tell us his/her own thoughts as to the reason they have come for counseling. Shirley began:

> "Well, I am not having "real" orgasms. I have been doing some reading lately about sex and orgasms. I found out that I am missing out on a lot. The orgasms I have been having are not the right kind. I want to have an orgasm with penile thrusting."

Sam:

> "Frankly, I do not understand why we are here. I thought our 'sex life' was fantastic. She has orgasms with various kinds of stimulation and has always seemed to really enjoy them. She, in fact, has orgasms during intercourse! I just don't understand."

Shirley:

> "That is true. I do have orgasms during intercourse, but you are either caressing my clitoris, kissing my breasts or doing something else and that is cheating! According to my interpretation of what I have read, I should be able to just lie there and have orgasms just by your penis thrusting inside my vagina!"

Having either vaginal or clitoral orgasms is not an index of the sexually responsive female. This notion is about as valid as saying that one position of intercourse is "better" than another. Better for whom? Better for everybody or just for people living east of the Rockies?

What about the females who can experience orgasms with breast or anal stimulation or by caressing the small of the back or with fantasy? Where do they fit into the vaginal vs. clitoral controversy? The fact is that physiologically, orgasm by whatever means is an orgasm. Experience them in whatever way is best for you.

Orgasm Equals Satisfaction

For some husbands it is more important for his wife to have an orgasm for his sake than it is for her to have one for her own pleasure. In this situation the emphasis is on the husband's "performance" needs being met rather than the wife's sexual satisfaction. Apparently many wives have some trouble convincing their husbands that on occasions, they may thoroughly enjoy a sexual encounter but may not feel the desire to have orgasms. On these occasions, it is usually the husband who wants his wife to have an orgasm because:

1. This justifies his feeling of sexual pleasure and consequently his own orgasm.
2. He wants his wife to enjoy the sexual experience as much as he "thinks" he does, therefore, she has to have one also.
3. He would feel that he would not be getting the job done if she didn't.
4. His male ego needs it.

All of these may be partly true and important in the sexual adjustment of some couples because in our culture we tend to believe that having an orgasm is "satisfaction guaranteed." Orgasms have become the critical measure of sexual satisfaction for partners who have the attitude that the *purpose* or *goal* of all caressing, kissing, touching, and intercourse is to *obtain* an orgasm. However, we have found it is these same couples who often tell us: "Something has happened to our sex-life." For them even sex has lost its intimate potential. Physiological satisfaction may follow orgasm (or orgasms) but personal glow and interpersonal warmth do not necessarily follow.

Chapter 14

DIM Four: Sex Is Timing

There is a great deal of concern with *where* orgasms should be experienced (vaginal versus clitoral), *how* orgasms should be experienced (tasting, touching, thrusting), *how many* should be experienced, and *how quickly* orgasms should be experienced. We discussed the *where* and *how* of orgasms in the last chapter. The *how many* and *how quickly* aspects of orgasms deserve separate treatment because for many partners *sex is a matter of timing*. This is true in the literal sense.

Usually it is the husband's timing that catches the blame. He either: 1) ejaculates too fast, 2) cannot wait until after his wife has an orgasm, or 3) cannot have an orgasm at the same time his wife does. Of course, the wife is not entirely left out of the timing picture. The problem here is that it may take her "too long" to have an orgasm. Rare indeed is the complaint that the woman climaxes too soon! With some couples their timing problem can destroy any pleasure in the sexual encounter. The encounter becomes a battle ground for gratification that is largely controlled by the clock.

The physiological signs for both male and female sexual "readiness" occurs within the same length of time. That is, the woman's vaginal lubrication and the man's erection can occur within 10-30 seconds during the excitement phase of sexual arousal. So physiologically speaking both sexes may be "ready" at the same time. Ready for what? Intercourse maybe, but not necessarily orgasm.

Together Now: One, Two, Three!

If a couple believes having simultaneous orgasms is the ultimate sex experience and they fail to make it then several things are possible:

1. If the wife has an orgasm before her husband, she probably doesn't think it necessary to apologize for not "waiting" for him. However, she may feel disappointed that they didn't make it together.
2. If the husband ejaculates "too soon," the chances are he not only feels disappointed that he could not wait for her, but he will probably say so.
3. If the husband ejaculates "too soon," the wife will probably not express her disappointment, but will mumble something like, "That's O.K., honey—maybe next time."

If they make it together the process may be something like this:

Wife:
"I know he is getting ready. I wish I could hurry up. If only he would slow down a bit. I can tell by his breathing that he is about there. I can't excite him too much now or he will surely lose it. Oh, why doesn't he SLOW DOWN!"
Husband:
"I wonder where she is. I guess she is getting there because she looks like it. If only I could slow down a little bit and give her a chance to get caught up. Why doesn't she HURRY UP!"
Wife:
"Now honey."
Husband:
"Now?"
Wife:
"Now! Now!"
Husband:
"We made it!" (I guess she did.)

Wife:
(Sigh) "We made it."
Husband:
(Sigh)

Sex play and intimacy is not a matter of precise timing. Better all clocks were thrown away. Let's look at this from another point of view.

1. Simultaneous orgasms can be fun and different when they occur naturally during love-making.
2. To work on the exact timing of having orgasms together every time may well distract each partner from enjoying what's going on.
3. Not "making it" together can be an unnecessary source of frustration and resentment.
4. Orgasms are a very private, personal experience. During those few exquisite moments of pleasure, we are very much turned into ourself. There is good reason for this in that during the orgasmic phase there is a reduction of sensory input to the nervous system. In other words, we really do not see, feel, smell, hear, or taste as well during the orgasmic experience. Because of this very intense, private, and personal experience, the chances are that couples who are arriving at the orgasmic phase at the same time can not fully appreciate each other's orgasmic experience.
5. Orgasm does not just occur in the genitals, but is a *total* body response. The full awareness and appreciation of our partner's orgasmic experience can add considerably to the overall pleasures of the intimate encounter, thus it seems experiencing *sequential* orgasms is far more reasonable and pleasurable than working and worrying so much about timing.

The E-P-E Male

Not all partners are "Together Now: One, Two, Three" couples. Some are suffering (by their own admission) from what we call the Erection-Penetration-Ejaculation (E-P-E) syndrome. This simply means that as soon as the penis is erect, it is inserted into the vagina and within the shortest possible time it ejaculates. For some husbands, who by their very nature strive for efficiency, this may seem like a perfectly reasonable way to get the job done. But, of course "all work and no play. . . ."

It really depends on what you want—efficiency or ecstasy. For the husband to work so hard and furiously for the very thing that, at least temporarily, terminates his erotic pleasure has never made much sense. The male has a refractory period which follows his ejaculation during which time (this varies from man to man) he may not achieve a full erection nor have another ejaculation. In this sense, ejaculation for the male temporarily terminates his erotic pleasure. And, it is sad but true, usually the wife's as well because the typical Mr. "I've had mine" rolls over and goes to sleep.

Most men would prefer to get out of the E-P-E syndrome. It is more difficult to do than most wives realize, however. After all, males have had a tremendous amount of training and positive reinforcement in becoming an E-P-E expert. With the E-P-E syndrome, it might be enlightening for both husbands and wives to realize that this "condition" is not necessarily an intentional one but rather one that has come about through years of conditioning. For example, as a young boy, the male probably masturbated rapidly to avoid being "caught." In his early intercourse experiences in the back seat of a car, fear of being caught was probably again his primary motivation for rapidity of ejaculation, and if he by chance sought the services of prostitutes, rapidity again was the name of the game. Possibly the earlier years of marriage brought with it a naive bride who thought his E-P-E was a sure sign of how much she turned him on. She could have reinforced him admirably! All of this is past history, what can be done in the present?

The P-P-P

Suppose there was a mechanism similar to the refractory period which occurred *before* intercourse—a Pre-Penetration

Period (P-P-P) during which time intercourse was not possible for say 30 to 45 minutes. All of the other components of sexual arousal remain intact and functional, it is just during this period that actual intercourse must be postponed. How would you spend this time together?

With the pressure off to get on with "RT", undoubtedly both partners would learn to relax and to begin to appreciate the tremendous amount of intimate pleasure than can be enjoyed in and of itself. This kind of "restriction" would probably produce a lot of creativity that would insure both partners were thoroughly enjoying themselves and each other. We are not going to use the term *foreplay* as that has a goal orientation. What about excitement? Sexual excitement occurs when partners can take the time to kiss, caress, touch, massage, look at, tease, talk, and play with each other. The whole process becomes an enjoyable sharing where each partner can appreciate his or her sexual and erotic feelings. Being a part of this process without the urgency to "get down to business" can be one of the most pleasurable ways to be with each other.

If you decided to take a walk with each other, would you see how fast you could go? If you planned on a special meal at a restaurant, would it make any sense to see how fast you could eat it? Probably you would take your time to taste, look at, and smell each dish. Would you share your favorite dish with your partner? The best part of all of these shared moments is doing them together, not completing them.

What do you feel about becoming a connoisseur of sexual pleasure? There are so many pleasures that are available to all of us. There are wine connoisseurs, gourmet cooks, various collectors and hobbyists, all of whom have become experts through experience, practice, and knowledge. As married partners, we *each* can have the opportunity of becoming a sensual and sexual expert *with* each other. One of the first steps would be in slowing down and enjoying the process of becoming an expert. Of course, there is nothing wrong with a "quickie" every now and then. But if this is all that ever happens, then there is room (and time) for improvement.

Tune In—Not Out

Males have a two-stage ejaculation which is both subjectively and physiologically differentiated. For a few seconds, the male feels that he is about to ejaculate and this is quickly followed by the propulsion of semen out of the penis. Ejaculation occurs in the male genital system while the pleasurable subjective feelings of orgasm occur in the brain. It is possible for a male to ejaculate and not have the feelings of orgasm (for example, in some spinal cord injured males) or to have an orgasm but not to ejaculate (for example, in the male who has ejaculated a few times in a short period of time and has exhausted his supply of semen).

Ejaculating too quickly is usually not a problem when a male masturbates or is orally and/or manually stimulated by his partner. The problem usually occurs with penis-in-vagina intercourse. This is certainly a legitimate complaint if both partners would like intercourse to last longer at times. Here are some ways:

1. Slow down. Vary the speed and depth of thrusting.
2. Stop. Just stop thrusting all together now and then and enjoy the sensation of the penis in the vagina.
3. Take it out. Continue with other play activities. After a few moments or minutes of play insert the penis into the vagina again. Do this off and on several times.

Now, slowing down, stopping, taking it out, or a combination of these probably doesn't sound like an earth shaking solution but it may help to break into the E-P-E syndrome. Incidentally, another way to last longer is to simply increase the frequency of sexual touches leading to and including ejaculation. If this difficulty persists and is a matter of concern by either partner, we suggest you seek effective treatment methods employed by qualified sex therapists.

I Would Like Another—And Another

Women have no refractory period, thus, after one orgasm they are capable of another and another and another—with no time limitation. This is one of the few differences in the male and female sexual systems. This difference is either delightful or disastrous, depending on what you think about it and, more importantly, what you *do* about it.

Disastrous if you believe the following:

1. It is the husband's responsibility to *give* his wife an orgasm.
2. The only correct way to have an orgasm is with the penis in the vagina during intercourse.
3. Penile thrusting is a necessary and/or sufficient stimulus for a woman's orgasm.
4. Orgasm is necessary for satisfaction.
5. One orgasm is always enough.
6. Too many orgasms will weaken your moral fiber.
7. A woman *should* have more than one orgasm.
8. "Nice" women never have more than one orgasm.
9. Your husband should be able to read your mind and know when none, one, two, three, etc. orgasm(s) is not enough.
10. Orgasm is not a natural consequence of sexual excitement/arousal, but rather, something which with experience and concentrated effort is simply a matter of timing (Together Now: One, Two, Three).

Delightful, if you believe none of the above and both of you are willing to behaviorally explore the full circle of intimacy with each other.

Chapter 15

DIM Five: Sex Is Sex

Always and Always

Most people would agree that "variety is the spice of life." Yet, when it comes to sex in marriage a prevailing attitude is "sex is sex." This attitude is exemplified by the couple's behavior. Usually in describing their "sex life" many couples began each sentence with "We always have . . . ." For example:

"We always have . . .
sex on Sunday."
sex in the dark."
sex in the morning."
sex in the bedroom."
sex at night."
sex with the husband on top."
sex with the lights on."
sex after a fight."
sex every night at 10:00."
sex on our anniversary."
sex on the living room floor."
sex on New Year's Eve."
sex with our clothes on."
sex nude."

She Always . . .

I can tell when she wants sex because she always . . .

tells me.
wears her blue nightie.
prepares my favorite meal.
lights the candles.
starts a fight.
calls me a pet name.
runs my bath water.
asks me if I want sex.
blows in my ear.
says she is going to bed to read.

He always . . .

I can tell when he wants sex because he always . . .

shaves after dinner.
gives me a special look.
tells me he loves me.
pinches my breasts.
takes out the garbage.
drinks a six-pack.
brings me a surprise.
tells me it's been a week.
asks me if I'm in the mood.
turns on the stereo.

Is It Worth the Catch?

When he takes the bait, I know what will happen next—step by step—because he always . . .

tells me to take my clothes off.
puts his arms around me and pats my fanny.
gives me a peck on the lips.
grabs my breasts.
plunges into intercourse.
rolls over and says, "Well, honey, how was that?"

When she takes the bait, I know what will happen next—step by step—because she always . . .

tells me to go take a shower.
kisses my nose.

asks me if I love her.
turns off the light.
asks if the children are *really* asleep.
rolls over and says, "That was nice, honey."

You Can Depend on Us

Another routine couple: We like variety, therefore, we always . . .

hang the mirror over the bed.
undress each other.
mutually fondle breast and genitals for ten minutes.
take a shower together.
use the vibrator for 7 minutes.
have intercourse for 4 minutes.
tell each other how great it was.
share our fantasies.
go to sleep.

Nothing seems to be quite so deadly dull as when both partners *always* know on a moment-by-moment basis what is going to happen next. This can range from the time and place, to who makes the first move and all of the subsequent ones.

Hi, Honey, It's Wednesday

For most of these couples physical intimacy gradually evolves into a specific sex routine. For other couples, the problems of when and how to have sex became so great that various "specific agreements" are worked out.

Example:

Hal and Hazel had been married nine years. They had always had a problem with who initiates sex and how to fit it into their busy schedules. Hal sometimes worked late into the evenings and Hazel's responsibilities included a part-time job and taking care of the three children. They both enjoyed sex but usually one or both were "too tired" or "not in the mood" during the rare free time they had together. Over the years they developed a little game to check each other out to see if sex was on the agenda that evening. Usually this ended up in

> more resentment and frustrations than it did pleasure, so they agreed on a plan. Since all other aspects of their lives were "programmed," they reasoned that sex could be as well. They agreed on Wednesday night as their night for sex. Unless something quite unusual happened they knew they would have sex on Wednesday night. It made little or no difference if one or both were unusually tired. It also made no difference if one or both didn't want sex. After all, this was an agreement and both were determined to meet their commitment. Most of the time the agreement worked because Hal and Hazel could at least look forward to getting down to business on Wednesday night. This knowledge helped to reduce a lot of tensions and also cut out the game-playing.

When this couple came in for counseling it was not specifically the Wednesday-night-sex routine that was giving them trouble. Both agreed this arrangement was far better than anything else they had tried over the past nine years. Each believed the other was a fantastic sex partner. Yet, something was wrong. Something was missing. Even their *good* penis-in-vagina sex with its foreplay and afterglow has lost its intimate potential.

Hal and Hazel wanted more relatedness and meaningfulness in their relationship. They had lost touch with themselves and each other. Wednesday night was no exception.

Whether physical intimacy gradually evolves into a specific "sex routine" or it becomes routine by "specific agreement" really makes no difference as far as the consequences are concerned. For, in either situation, there is a subsequent loss of "special person" feelings. Without these feelings vitalizing intimacy in marriage becomes nothing more than a weak attempt to add one more rung to the ladder of sex.

Something Old, Something New

"Special person" feelings go hand-in-hand with behaviors. We have defined intimacy as circles of behaviors that can be shared, expressed, and appreciated on a moment-by-moment basis. These behaviors include experimenting with something new: a different position for intercourse, a vibrator, a different food, a waterbed, a game of tennis, and anything you both would like to try. The circles also include doing something that is not so new: holding hands, a genital caress, an I-message, a smile, and anything that says "I love you, *now*." With the circles nothing is programmed—nothing has to be. There are no steps, no phases, no rituals. Everything is possible and far from routine.

Sex in marriage can be a "celebration" of two people who are in a loving relationship. It can be a renewing, almost "transcendental experience." It can be a source of inspiration. It can give depth and meaningfulness to the relationship. It can be a "spiritual union" and a "celestial soaring." It can be all of this and much, much more, but the sex experience is more than *symbolic*. Sex is also designed to be fun and pleasurable. There is absolutely nothing *wrong* with enjoying sexual intimacy in marriage. It is a free transaction between married partners that creates this enjoyment. The body is a fantastic instrument of pleasure. It simply needs to be played.

When you play tennis, play cards, play a musical instrument, play anything (or play *with* anything), you are involved, creative, and, most of all, you enjoy what you are doing. This is why the term "sex play" is so appropriate. It means that married partners can play *with* each other because it is fun, exciting, and particularly meaningful. You may play with your partner's body because *you* enjoy it; *you* can be creative and imaginative because *you* are involved in what *you* are doing. Of course, your partner may thoroughly enjoy "receiving" this attention, but as a *player* it is possible to be quite involved in what *you* are doing for *your own* satisfaction and pleasure as well as your partner's.

This can be a very meaningful and insightful experience for many partners who may never have thought of their partners' bodies as something that *they* could enjoy playing with. A recent example was a wife who came back for a follow-up interview and exclaimed how excited she was with her newfound "toy." For years she had stimulated her husband's penis because she knew that *he* enjoyed it, but in all of that time she never realized how much enjoyment *she* could have, just playing with it. It's all a matter of attitude.

The secret to learning to play with each other is realizing the freedom to explore the circles of intimacy.

Part IV
The Intimate Adventure

Chapter 16

It Is the Behaviors That Count

In the previous two sections, we explored some of the prevalent ideas that many husbands and wives have about marriage, sex, and intimacy. We have suggested that marriage, sex, and intimacy are perhaps more or different than what you may have thought. We have found these suggestions useful in helping couples in their process of vitalizing the intimacy that is potentially theirs to share in marriage. Since the *VIM* approach to this process has been rewarding to so many marriages we would like to review some of the main points presented thus far.

A Summary

Some of the attitudes that often restrict the intimate potential of the marriage relationship are:

1. Marriage will naturally take care of itself.
2. Boredom is a natural consequence of marriage.
3. We are married—we are one.
4. Now that we are married, we have all the time in the world.
5. We are not lovers anymore, we are married.

Some of the attitudes which often restrict the intimate potential of sex are:

1. Sex=Intercourse=Intimacy
2. Sex is something you do to or do for your partner.
3. Sex is having orgasms.
4. Sex is timing.
5. Sex is sex.

We believe that some of these attitudes, or variations of them, occur in a great many marriages. In the next ten years as marital health becomes a focus for research and good information finds its way into the educational process, these prevalent attitudes will have less influence on what constitutes intimacy between married partners. But it is not ten years from now, it is now. *VIM* is written to and for the married couple who wish to explore for themselves an expanded intimacy now. To help you in this process *VIM* takes a three-step approach by:

1. Identifying some of the attitudes which may be blocking the exploration.
2. Presenting alternatives to these attitudes which may be more personally and interpersonally meaningful and pleasurable.
3. Suggesting specific behaviors that you can incorporate into your own creative process of experiencing intimacy in marriage.

In this sense, *VIM* is another "how to" book but with a different focus. *VIM* is an approach to developing intimacy in marriage which has evolved from our Pairing Enrichment Program (PEP) and the follow-up feedback we have received from several hundred PEP participants. It has also evolved from our own marriage and the significant changes that have occurred with our own attitudes on marriage, sex, and intimacy.

Many of the "how to" books are designed at improving sex techniques and having bigger orgasms and better sex more often. The *VIM* approach in no way detracts from the importance of combating sexual monotony with learning as many variations of a theme as possible. Creativity is the essence of these books as well as of *VIM*. The difference is that, rather than focusing on sex, *VIM* explores the pleasures of an expanded intimacy.

We have defined intimacy as a circle of unending behaviors which can be freely shared and appreciated simply for what they are: an important moment with each other. This includes such a wide range of behaviors that it is probably somewhat presumptuous to make a list, however, it may be helpful to try. There is no order in this sequence and some of these may be unfamiliar until described in subsequent chapters.

Communicating with I-messages.
A face caress.
An unexpected kiss.
Leaving a note for your partner to find.
A walk in the woods.
Making a "date" with your partner.
Cuddling up in bed "greeting" in the morning.
Bathing each other.
Candlelight dinner.
Holding hands.
A foot caress.
A full body hug.
A genital caress or touch.
Planning a trip together.
A surprise gift.
Playing a game together.
Getting dressed up just for your partner.
An unexpected "I love you."
A body caress.
"Just thinking about you" telephone call.
Sexual intercourse.
Sharing a positive feeling.
A real compliment.
A playful touch.
Showing your appreciation.
An erotic touch.
Noticing something special about your partner.
Exploring personal ideas together.
A touch anywhere that feels good to you.
Laughing together.
Giving your partner information about yourself.

Watching tv together—touching.
Touching each other while driving together.
A secretive touch.
Getting undressed together at an unusual time.
That special look at your partner.
Telling your partner how good you feel.
Partially undressing your partner so that you can touch special places.
Bringing your partner coffee to bed.
Doing "chores" together but making it an intimate occasion.
Communicating about the relationship.
A hobby together.
Listening for each other's return home and greeting partner.
Planning for that special night together when there are no other plans.
Asking your partner to touch or caress you when and where you would like.
Bringing your partner a flower from the yard.
Showing your partner how you like to be touched or caressed with I-movements.
Helping your partner without asking or being asked.
Supporting each other at times when needed.

As you can see, no list can do justice to intimacy because this includes just about anything and everything that partners find personally meaningful to do together—or rather to do *with* each other. This may differ from couple to couple but everything on this list is a potential intimate encounter. *Intimacy is generated and created by two special people seeing each other as special partners sharing something special with each other.*

If you read over the list carefully you probably noticed that some items could be classified as "physical" intimacy involving touch, while others were "non-physical." Many of these touching behaviors are often considered as "foreplay" which, for some couples, invariably leads to another one of the intimacies—sexual intercourse. We suggest that everything around the intimacy circle is under voluntary conscious control and can consequently be initiated at will. It is this "willing" intimacy to happen that makes a special and unique situation between married partners. In this interchange, each partner becomes significant with the other. "Giving" your partner a genital caress or touch differs only in degree from "giving" your partner a flower. A natural consequence of each may be that a genital caress may include erotic feelings and an orgasm. A sniff of a flower may include special person feelings and a sneeze. In both cases by "giving" you are really sharing yourself intimately with your partner in a special way. The two examples definitely differ in intensity and emotional context but both can also be appreciated just for what they are.

Here is another example: A genital kiss is no different in many ways than a kiss on your partner's ear. Both may tickle, both may be erotic, and both may be fun for both partners. The difference between the two has to do usually with when they are given. An ear kiss can be playful and mean nothing in particular, while a genital kiss may be interpreted as "serious" and mean something definite (if you are climbing the ladder). Once again, we certainly realize that the two kisses are quite different but this serves to make the point that anything around the intimacy circle may be pleasurable, enjoyed by both partners, and serves to celebrate the uniqueness and meaningfulness of the *process* on the relationship. Intimacy, in effect, signifies the very *existence of this process.*

Married couples who are motivated to enrich their personal and interpersonal experiences within a loving and free relationship find that they can do no wrong when exploring all of the dimensions of intimacy together. The attitude that "I can do nothing wrong" in sharing intimately with my partner is a very freeing experience. It not only permits change and growth to occur within the relationship but it acknowledges and reaffirms each partner's self-esteem and self-appreciation. Freeing up this type of intimacy often takes practice and time. It does not come easy for some couples who find it awkward to be "intimate" with each other beyond an occasional sexual encounter.

Sometimes we put so many unnecessary restrictions on our enjoyment of being with each other in special and meaningful ways. So many of these restrictions come from our past. There was the wife who said that her husband never held her hand in public yet she would enjoy that experience.

On the few occasions when they had held hands she had "good feelings." We asked him what his feelings were and found out:

1. He was teased by his classmates as a child when "caught" holding his girl friend's hand.
2. It signified to the public that he was a "mushy," sentimental type person. It was not the "masculine" thing to do.
3. It might embarrass other people who saw them because it has sexual overtones and "affection is a private affair."

A marriage relationship is made up of two individual and unique people who have gathered a tremendous amount of historical data before they even met. A great deal of this information may no longer be appropriate or even desirable as far as the *new* experience of the marriage *partnership* is concerned. The emphasis on this third entity—the *relationship*—and all of the wealth of knowledge that continuously evolves from it would seem to be a better reference point for exploring intimacy. With the "hand-holding" couple, we asked that at the next opportunity he reach out for her hand with the idea that this was symbolic of nothing more than an experience of the *relationship*. We shared with him the idea of expanding intimacy in marriage and the significance intimacy has in marriage. Getting this couple to hold hands in public was not the real point. We learned much later:

> "You know it may sound strange but that simple act of holding hands in public really started me thinking. I began to wonder about all of the other areas of our relationship that I was neglecting because of some stupid reasons that don't make any sense. I mean it might make sense to *me* but it doesn't make any sense for *us*."

The three important elements in marriage are me-you-us. It is the *us* that is sometimes neglected or not given the free range that is so essential for maintaining the enriching experience of marriage.

Let's look at another example. This couple had been

married for twenty-two years. During these years, their "sex script" had taken one form. This was dictated by two primary DIM's. On her part, she firmly believed that the only proper way for her to have an orgasm was with P-in-V intercourse (DIM 3). The few times she had experienced orgasm with her husband by manual or oral caressing had left her feeling terribly guilty. The husband's DIM was that he was definitely responsible for his wife's pleasure and orgasms (DIM 2). If, as usually happened, he did ejaculate before she experienced an orgasm during intercourse he would suppress any reaction to his orgastic pleasure and try to continue with his thrusting until her climax. As a result she never really knew exactly when he had an orgasm or, more importantly, if he *enjoyed* the experience. Each wanted the other to loosen up and enjoy sex more. At the same time, they wished this also for themselves. Why then didn't they just get together, talk it over, and try some new potentially intimate behaviors? Because it often takes a lot of VIM to counteract twenty-two years of DIM's. He would say, for example, that he would really like to be a little more selfish on occasions and just be "done unto." But "all of his life" he had thought that it was his job to satisfy his wife. She had learned that sex which was equated with P-in-V, was the only acceptable form of intimacy.

This couple wanted to expand the total range of intimacy that they could share together. Although it was a gradual process for them, they found that experiencing new behaviors helped them to restructure some of the old DAM's and DIM's into more productive attitudes about intimacy; it is truly the behaviors that count! They began to explore the behaviors on all three of the circles of intimacy (Special Person, Sensory and Erotic) on a day-by-day basis without invariably climbing the ladder. They became more attentive and appreciative of each other and each felt special to the other. They really were becoming lovers again for they were caring for each other lovingly.

In the remaining chapters we will share with you a few of the behaviors that couples have found effective in opening up a new and more fulfilling, exciting intimacy for them. We realize that all couples are at different places in their marriage. This is particularly true where "intimacy" is concerned. Vitalizing intimacy in marriage is a very personal experience. In fact, each married couple *creates* the type of intimacy that is meaningful for them. Consequently it is the process rather than the content that we are most interested in. The fact that you have reached this point in *VIM* is probably a good indication that you want to do something potentially constructive in your relationship. Therefore, we are structuring an experiential format for the two of you to follow. Because we strongly believe that intimacy is created by two unique partners in their unique relationship, these suggestions can best be described as a catalyst in this process. It takes two special people communicating *with* each other in a special relationship that allows intimacy and growth to occur. An important part of this process involves attitude and commitment.

By attitude we mean a genuine desire to begin to discover something new in yourself and your partner. This involves a willingness to put aside many of the old unproductive ways you have related to or for your partner and begin to share yourself *with* your partner. In other words, in order to discover something, you have to explore. In order to explore, you must have an attitude that you really do not know everything about your partner and learning can be an adventure.

By commitment we mean that *both* of you as individuals are committed to making the very most of your present relationship. This means that you are *both* committed to the *changing process* of your partnership. It is really not up to one of you to change and grow but with each partner helping the other then two people have the opportunity of growing together. In the process the marriage becomes dynamic and enriched. The process of VIM facilitates individual growth *through* the relationship.

Some Guidelines

If the two of you are familiar with VIM to this point and wish to follow the experiential format, then we suggest you follow these guidelines:

1. Share the next chapter called "Being Aware" by reading it together. Follow the suggestions as they occur.
2. Try not to think about this as "homework" or something that you have to get done in exactly the way it is presented. A much better approach would be to develop your own creativity in incorporating these exercises and suggestions into your own relationship. One of the biggest problems often encountered is not "finding" enough time together. Initially "making" time to be together may be the only solution. Hopefully the suggestions will be meaningful for both of you. If they are, the chances are that you will *want* to experience more of them with each other.
3. You might want to experience one chapter in an evening or follow one or two suggestions in the chapter during a week. Set your own pace.
4. Remember the purpose of the remainder of *VIM* is to offer you the opportunity to think, talk and do something about vitalizing intimacy in your own unique relationship with each other. Obviously you may feel that some of the exercises are more relevant than others. We encourage you to try all of them. Some you may wish to do more than one time. Hopefully, the total process will enable you to develop your own creativity in continually exploring the dimension of intimacy in your marriage. *VIM* is only a beginning.
5. Follow these general guidelines for the remaining chapters on Being Authentic, Being Free, and Being Secure.
6. Before you start, we suggest that each of you look over the list of DAM's and DIM's and pick those that you would especially like to work on in your marriage.

Sometimes just becoming aware of DAM's and DIM's is helpful in breaking them. However, for most couples it requires more than that. For many, it entails a three-step process:

1. Awareness
2. Communication
3. Behavioral Change

The first step is obviously necessary for you can't change something if you are not aware of its existence. The second step suggests that you can't do it alone. You need your partner's help and understanding. And indeed you do. The third step is perhaps the most difficult one for it requires *doing* in addition to thinking and talking; it requires risking.

This section on the Intimate Adventure is designed to help you with all three of these important steps, one chapter builds upon the next.

Let's begin.

Chapter 17

Being Aware

In this chapter we want to explore the awareness of feelings related to ourselves, our partner, and our relationship. We want to begin to build on here-and-now experiences and feelings.

First Remember

The range of feelings that we can experience on a moment-by-moment basis is tremendous. Just a few of them are:

Sadness	Fear
Love	Loneliness
Shame	Tenderness
Sex	Anger
Guilt	Boredom
Joy	Silliness
Anxious	Hurt
Frustration	Excitement
Embarrassment	Happiness

Suggestion

Remember some events in your relationship. When both of you are ready read the first statement, then just think about it for a while. After this, share your thoughts with your partner and then share the feeling(s) you are experiencing *now*. Go to the next statement and do the same. The point of this exercise is to get in touch with and share feelings, *not* to point out errors (or so you may think) in your partner's memory.

1. Think about the first time you talked with each other. What were your feelings then?
2. Think of the things that pleased you most about this person?
3. What were the things that pleased you most about yourself at that time?
4. Think about your decision to marry. What motivated you to select this person to be your spouse?
5. What did you expect your marriage to be like?
6. Think about the most meaningful sexual experiences that you have had with your spouse. Try to think of the reasons why they were so meaningful to you.

Were you able to identify and take ownership of your own feelings? Once you identified certain feelings could you express them clearly and openly to your partner? What about the person you married. Do *you* think that your relationship is one where your *partner* feels free enough to express all of his/her feelings? Are there some that you have trouble with? Are there some that you wish your partner would express to you more often? All of this is a part of being aware. Being aware of *yourself* and experiencing your *self-in-relationship* with your partner can be one of the most important factors in allowing the marriage to be a dynamic relationship.

The variety of feelings that we have and the way we share these feelings with our partner can provide a rich source of meaning and excitement for the relationship to build on. On the other hand, feeling stiffled because: "It's not right for me to feel this way!" or "My spouse does not want me to feel this way" offers nothing to continuing to communicate effectively. Indeed it blocks communication because you are simply not allowing yourself to be—yourself. You are not responsible for the feelings you have. They occur in response to a variety of situations. You are, however, responsible for what you do with those feelings.

The "Familiar" Partner

How you feel about yourself and how you feel about your partner is a constantly *changing* process. We are different persons and different partners at different times. This offers us the opportunity of continually discovering and rediscovering our familiar partner in a different way on a moment-by-moment basis.

Suggestion

Discuss this concept with each other for a moment. Are you aware that your familiar partner is a person that you really do not know? How can you help him or her discover the newness in you?

Suggestion

Below is a list of 15 bipolar terms with seven numbered spaces in between each pair. Each of you go through this list one at a time and write down the number (on a separate piece of paper) that corresponds to your "place" on the continuum as you see yourself in *relationship with your partner.*

As you do this think to yourself, "I see myself now as—" then jot the number down. For example, if you see yourself as 100 percent pessimistic you would mark "1" or 100 percent optimistic you would mark "7" in relation with your partner. If you see yourself as completely neutral, then you would mark "4." Of course, you can mark in any of the blanks.

When you both have finished take a pencil and mark each of your responses in the book. One of you might choose an "X" mark and the other an "O".

Go over each set of terms and discuss any similarities or differences that you may have. Discuss your choices. *Note:*

Do not argue about specific points. Try to get in touch with how you feel *accepting* the way your partner sees himself or herself in the relationship.

I see myself now as:

	1	2	3	4	5	6	7	
PESSIMISTIC								OPTIMISTIC
COLD								WARM
RIGID								FLEXIBLE
STIMULATING								UNSTIMULATING
UNPLEASANT								PLEASANT
EXCITING								UNEXCITING
UNATTRACTIVE								ATTRACTIVE
UNSELFISH								SELFISH
UNIMPORTANT								IMPORTANT
INTERESTING								BORING
UNINHIBITED								INHIBITED
CLOSED								OPEN
AGGRESSIVE								PASSIVE
TENSE								RELAXED
ATTENTIVE								UNATTENTIVE

You may have had some pleasant surprises and learned something interesting from this experience. On the other hand you may have been disappointed in a few of your partner's choices. This can be a positive experience also. It is O.K. to express disappointment because you are giving information, but it is quite another thing if you ended up trying to convince your partner that he or she really does not feel that way or should not feel that way. Of course, that can lead you nowhere because you simply cannot legislate feelings or take all the responsibility for how your partner should or should not feel.

The most important thing to realize from this experience is that the marks you have placed can shift from moment to moment depending on your experience in the relationship. Your marriage is in constant movement because you are constantly changing both as a person and as a partner. If you repeated this exercise tomorrow or next week, the chances are the marks would shift to the right or left a little. We are indeed evolving, changing people in our partnership.

How you feel about yourself depends on a lot of things including how you feel about your partner. This does not mean that this is the way your partner really is but it is your *perception* of your partner on a moment-by-moment basis.

Suggestion

Below is a list of the same bipolar terms. Follow the same instructions as before except this time respond to the way you see *your partner now*. When you have placed both of your marks on the sheet then discuss this experience. This is an exercise where you can share information about the interaction between the me, you, and us in marriage.

I see my partner now as:

	1	2	3	4	5	6	7	
PESSIMISTIC	__	__	__	__	__	__	__	OPTIMISTIC
COLD	__	__	__	__	__	__	__	WARM
RIGID	__	__	__	__	__	__	__	FLEXIBLE
STIMULATING	__	__	__	__	__	__	__	UNSTIMULATING
UNPLEASANT	__	__	__	__	__	__	__	PLEASANT
EXCITING	__	__	__	__	__	__	__	UNEXCITING
UNATTRACTIVE	__	__	__	__	__	__	__	ATTRACTIVE
UNSELFISH	__	__	__	__	__	__	__	SELFISH
UNIMPORTANT	__	__	__	__	__	__	__	IMPORTANT

INTERESTING	_ _ _ _ _ _ _ _ _	BORING
UNINHIBITED	_ _ _ _ _ _ _ _ _	INHIBITED
CLOSED	_ _ _ _ _ _ _ _ _	OPEN
AGGRESSIVE	_ _ _ _ _ _ _ _ _	PASSIVE
TENSE	_ _ _ _ _ _ _ _ _	RELAXED
ATTENTIVE	_ _ _ _ _ _ _ _ _	UNATTENTIVE

How you see your partner right now may not be the way you perceive him/her ten minutes from now.

In a marriage, the primary variable that produces change in how you see yourself and your partner is the *relationship*.

Growing Individually Together

In a growing marriage, two people can work together on their relationship *because* they can appreciate that they are two separate and unique individuals. Differing impressions, views and ideas can lead to some unexpected insights because we can learn something new about ourselves *and* our partners. Provided, that is, that each partner can really listen to the other without having to necessarily *agree* or *disagree* or be *right* or *wrong*. Married partnerships do not grow by proving points or convincing and coercing each other. They develop because the net result of experiencing the here-and-now transaction in the relationship permits two unique people to *grow individually together*.

Suggestion

Discuss this concept for a moment. What does it mean for each of you to "grow individually together."

Touch Opportunities

Hopefully marriage is a fun place to grow and experience. Sometimes the fun times are loose, free, and unscheduled times. At other times, they may result from planning and scheduling. In any event, sharing good times and having pleasurable feelings in the relationship always acknowledges that very special feature of your partnership. This is one of identity and intimacy.

Being Aware also involves a special sharing in marriage. Physical intimacy is something most humans need. This is *especially* true in marriage. Physical intimacy is simply communicating in another way. The same rules for good communication still apply.

For the next few suggestions, you have only *one* responsibility. It is a very important responsibility. That is to focus on your own sensations and feelings. Try to stay in touch with what is going on in you. Try not to distract yourself from this process by wondering what your partner is feeling, or wondering if he/she is really enjoying the experience. You may wish to tell your partner what you are feeling and that is fine. However, for now, that is not as important as really staying with the sensations and feelings you are experiencing.

Suggestion

Sometimes a lot of interesting feelings are generated when we bathe each other. These might include being cared for or feeling silly or awkward. The purpose here is not to get clean but to experience feelings of being with each other. Get into the tub or shower and wash each other. Wash every part of the other person. Take your time. Relax. Feel the hot water. Feel the soap as it goes over your partner's skin. Play. When you are finished, dry each other.

Suggestion

Apply a body lotion to your hands and massage your partner's feet. Squeeze the toes. Gently apply pressure to the sole of the foot, particularly the arch. Gently caress the top and bottom and sides of the foot simultaneously with both hands. Communicate. Take as little or as long as you like being the giver and the receiver. Focus on your own sensations and feelings both as "giver" and "receiver."

What have you shared in these encounters? Perhaps being with and being aware. Talk with each other about your own feelings.

Chapter 18

Being Authentic

Being authentic in marriage is learning to communicate effectively. There are obviously a lot of times when we are not authentic. For example, we may smile and say "I'm angry" or clench our fist and yell "I'm not angry." We are saying one thing and our tone of voice or body language is telling something else.

Communicating our true feelings *always* involves some risks. Have you ever had a feeling of closeness or tenderness toward your partner but because you were not willing to risk rejection you communicated indifference or even embarrassment?

Things That Please

It seems that there is a lot more risk involved in expressing positive ideas, feelings, or behaviors than the negative ones. For example, you might be driving home from work and thinking, "I bet the bicycle is in the driveway again" or "He/she has probably spent all our money on another one of those sales." Even before the first encounter of the day, we often prime ourselves with problems and negative feelings.

Before your marriage and early in the marriage, you probably took a great amount of pride in noticing the special things about your partner that particularly pleased you. For example: "I like the way you smile." "You really have some great ideas." "Your body feels so good to me." You were treating each other as special people.

It was important to you to let your partner know these things *and* it was important to your partner to hear these things. After all, our self-concept is based in large part on the feedback we get from people who are especially meaningful to us. Self-esteem and self-worth are important aspects of the relationship.

These positive thoughts and feelings may occur more often now but perhaps you may have let the opportunity pass to say anything about them more often. It could be that you are afraid to say something nice to your partner because you would be misunderstood. After all, your partner may think, "I wonder what he/she is up to?" "Does she want a special favor?" "Is he planning a fishing trip?" "What is he/she feeling guilty about?" etc. If this is the case, you may have gotten out of practice because you are taking the *relationship* for granted.

It is important to start *looking* for the things your spouse has *said* or *done* that please you and *communicate* these feelings rather than taking every opportunity to always criticize, reprimand, manipulate, and scold.

Suggestion

Sit facing each other, knee to knee, and hold hands. Take turns and tell your partner three things that please you most about him/her. Be authentic.

I-Messages

You probably started off your marriage by saying, "I do" to each other. Then, with some couples, this I-statement gets changed into "You don't—," "You never—," or "You always—" type of accusations. Accusing usually leads to defending and this always blocks communication.

A much better approach would be to go back to the I-message. These types of messages are an important and even essential way to keep communication open.

When you use I-messages you are taking ownership of your own feelings and taking responsibility for yourself in the relationship. I-messages give each partner the opportunity of representing *self* and to communicate directly with the security that you are accepted.

Saying things like "I feel—," "I would like—," "I don't like—," "I want to—," etc. gives your partner information.

By using I-messages you are not only giving each other information but if there is something that does not appeal to you then you have the opportunity of offering your *preference*. Feeling free enough to say "no" is important but it also helps to contribute your own preference. Incidentally, feeling free enough to say, "Yes, that's a great idea," is also important.

There are so many situations where not using I-messages leads to some of the most ambiguous situations.
A classic example is:

"Do you want sex tonight?"

What information does this convey to you? The sender of this message might be just taking a census! Even if the receiver was feeling sexual, this kind of message could well be a turnoff.

Of course, what the message could mean: "I don't want to take full responsibility for my sexual feelings particularly if I don't know where I am or where you are. I will ask you, then if you say, 'Yes' and I don't really want to, then I can say, 'You sure don't act like it' or something to that effect. If you say, 'No' then I'm off the hook and can finally go to sleep thinking that the reason we are not having sex tonight is your fault—as usual."

It can get complicated.

There are many ways that we avoid taking responsibility for ourselves in the relationship. For example:

"You drive me to drink" is different and more common than: "I drink too much."

"*You* make me angry" is often safer than: "I am angry."

Taking responsibility for our feelings, ideas, and attitudes, and expressing this to our partner with I-messages is certainly a part of Being Authentic. Perhaps the most important part.

Suggestion

Sit knee to knee, lean forward, and touch each other. This is a new and different person sitting before you. Part of the excitement about a marriage is the continuous rediscovery of each other if you take the time to listen and explore.

This is an exercise in sending I-messages.

Look at your partner and start a series of sentences which describe what you actually see. For example, you might say I see your blue eyes or I see you smiling. Take turns and stop after four "I-see" sentences.

Now start a new series of sentences with "I-feel." Tell your partner how you are feeling right now. Take four turns each.

Finally, take turns back and forth telling each other four things that you like. These "I-like" sentences can be about anything at all that you particularly like about yourself (I like the way I—), your partner (I like the way you—), or your relationship (I like the way we—).

Talk for a minute about how necessary it is to use I-messages in your relationship.

I-language gives your partner information but it is not meant to be demanding. For example.

"I want steak tonight, therefore, I'm going to get it!" is hardly constructive communication.

I-messages keep communication moving.

You-language can often block communication.

There is a big difference between: "You don't know how to kiss" and "I wish you would kiss me differently."

The you-statement is in the form of an accusation which will probably bring on defending and a block to communication. The I-statement stands a good chance of keeping the communication open provided the receiver accepts the statement as an opportunity of learning something that his/her partner thinks important. Helping each other to clarify the meaning of something said is an important aspect of keeping communication open. Some couples have made an agreement for partners to help each other by saying, "Hey, can you put that in an I-message, please" if there is a boggle in communication.

My Good Feelings

Let's look over the familiar feelings that were listed in *Being Aware*. They were:

Sadness	Fear
Love	Lonliness
Shame	Tenderness
Sex	Anger
Guilt	Boredom
Joy	Silliness
Anxiety	Hurt
Frustration	Excitement
Embarrassment	Happiness

Suggestion

Each take a piece of paper and write two feelings that you like to experience in your relationship. Discuss your choices with each other.

It is important that each of you help the other in understanding everything you can about these feelings. Such as when you experience them and what you would like to do to experience them more often. Can you express them easily, and what is your partner's feelings when you do express them? In other words, communicate with each other about these feelings.

Remember to use I-messages.

One way to fully experience the relationship is to take ownership of your true feelings or attitudes and express them *authentically*. This type of communication involves risking and being vulnerable but it can also add realism, insight, and personal meaningfulness to the partnership. Not *being authentic* can lead to falseness and deceit or denial and defensiveness. Too much of these elements can cause the communication and personal growth to suffer.

My Other Feelings

Participation in a marriage relationship involves many different experiences and many different feelings. Obviously these experiences and feelings are not *all* pleasant or to our liking. There are perhaps some feelings that we do not like to have in our relationship. Let's realize that these feelings will occur. Now, what can be done about them? Being aware of these feelings is obviously the first step. Communicating about them authentically with your partner is the second step. The third step is asking for your partner's help in your efforts to understand and change your attitudes and behaviors related to this feeling.

Suggestion

Each of you separately go back over the list of feelings and pick two feelings that you do not like to experience in the relationship.

When you have done this, then communicate as authentically as you can about all of the aspects of these feelings. When do you experience them? Do you have any feelings about these feelings? Help each other in finding out as much as you can about these feelings. Give each other I-messages.

Next, discuss what each of you can do to help your partner with the feelings that he/she does not like to experience.

A part of marriage is helping each other because you help the relationship.

Touch Opportunities

Being *true* to ourselves may offer us the opportunity of experiencing "old" situations differently and new situations with openness. Being true to ourselves is being true to the other person. Try to focus on your own feelings and sensations whatever they might be. This holds for both the "giver" and "receiver."

Feel free to experiment. For example, you might try these exercises with the lights on and music playing. Perhaps you would prefer candlelight or light from the fireplace.

Suggestion

During these body caressing exercises the receiver should try to keep his/her eyes closed. Be open and let the effects of touching move throughout your body. Allow whatever happens to happen. Be aware and be authentic. Let your partner know if he or she is *not* touching right or *is* touching right from your point of view. What is important is feeling, not technique. Here are some suggestions which you first may want to read through completely. These are only guidelines which may be helpful. Above all, it is important to caress your partner the way you want to.

Take your time.
Do not include the genitals or breast in this caressing experience.
Use a body lotion if you would like and start by stroking your partner's back, shoulders, and neck.
Massage partner's hands with both of yours.
Stroke partner's arms with both of your hands.
Oil and massage the feet.
Move up your partner's legs. Use wringing movements across the muscles of your partner's legs.
Stroke. Experiment. What feels good?
Stroke up the back side of your partner's legs up and over the buttocks.
Use pressure on either side of the legs as you move up.
Place your hands flat on your partner's lower back.
Use firm steady pressure and slide your hands up the back and across the shoulders. Use more oil as needed. Repeat.
Go across the small of your partner's back—from side to side.
Slide back and forth with hands going in opposite directions.
Move up slowly to shoulders. When you would like your partner to turn over say: "I would like you to turn over now."
Stroke the front of the body. Start at the abdomen.
Place your hands flat with fingers pointing down the side and

thumbs close together in the center of the body. Move up—with pressure—up and over the chest. Repeat several times. Communicate "I care" with your hands as you caress your partner's body.

Suggestion

For this face caress, you may want to sit or stand behind your partner's head. Move your fingers over your partner's forehead, cheeks, chin, nose, and mouth. If you are the receiver, you can place your hands on the giver's hands and show how you would like to have your face explored and caressed.

Move your partner's hand completely and show him or her what feels good. Use these I-movements often in all of the caressing exercises. With I-movements, you show your partner. With I-messages, you tell your partner. Both give valuable information about you as a special and changing person. Both help remove the "guessing game" approach. Both help put responsibility where it really belongs.

Take turns being the giver and receiver.

Try to experience this touch opportunity just for what it is. It is two people communicating intimately *with* each other. It is not "foreplay" or something you have to do to get to the "real thing." It may be simply appreciated as an intimate communication experience in and of itself.

It is particularly important to give each other information during all of the caressing experiences. Let your partner know what feels good or what might feel more pleasurable from your point of view. Remember that what feels good today may not tomorrow, so always communicate verbally or nonverbally just where you are.

Take turns inviting each other for a body, face, or foot caress during the next few days. Rather than asking your partner if he or she would like a caress put the statement in the form of an I-message. Give each other information.

Focus your attention on what is actually going on during this caressing experience.

Can you feel any different textures of your partner's body?

Are some parts of his or her body warmer than other parts?

Are some areas smooth and others rough?

What do you feel from your fingertips?

One last comment. It is certainly not the amount of time involved in these caressing experiences that is important. If, for one reason or another, time does not allow for a full body caress then it would be much better to concentrate on one or two particular parts of the body rather than hurriedly trying to cover every inch. On the other hand, *making* time to experience touching each other is important. If you want to experience this, then something must be done about it. It simply will not occur "naturally."

If you find these caressing experiences pleasurable then why not enjoy them more often?

Chapter 19

Being Free

Being free is an important aspect of a dynamic marriage. One of the factors which often gets in the way of being free is the marriage NOT's.

Marriage NOT's

Somewhere along the way we picked up a lot of notions about male/female roles and about things we should and should not do. Some of these notions are as valid as apple pie and others are destructive. Since most of these act to limit us, we call them NOT's. There are many NOT's concerning marriage.

For example:

Men do NOT need as much affection as women.
A good wife and mother does NOT work outside the home.
You must NOT ever trust a man.
Women do NOT want sex as much as men.
Lovemaking does NOT require information and communication; it will come naturally after marriage.
Satisfying sex is NOT mutual sharing, but rather, the husband's job and the wife's duty.
Children are the mother's responsibility, NOT the father's.
Partners should NOT intentionally hurt each other.
A husband does NOT cook. If he does, he is either a "sissy" or he is henpecked.

The husband is the provider and head of the house, NOT the wife.
The wife does NOT take out the garbage.
The husband does NOT vacuum the house.
A strong man does NOT show his emotions.

Certainly not all NOT's are bad or inappropriate. For example, "partners should NOT intentionally hurt each other" seems to be a very valid NOT. However, neither are they all necessarily appropriate for the way we may *want* to relate in marriage.

There is no doubt that these NOT's can have a powerful effect on our adult attitudes and behaviors. They may either consciously or unconsciously serve as guidelines for how we conceive a marriage "should" be. We may even feel intimidated because we think we *should* follow the NOT's even when we would like to *be free* enough not to.

Maintenance and Affectional Behaviors

Marriage can be divided into two types of activities. First are the *maintenance behaviors*. These are things like who pays the bills, makes repairs, goes shopping, prepares the meals, mows the grass, washes the clothes, cleans the house, makes the beds, etc., etc. Second are the *affectional behaviors*. These are things like showing appreciation, treating each other as special people, and sharing intimately with each other.

In other words, maintenance behaviors are necessary for the marriage as an economic-functioning unit and affectional behaviors serve to maintain the interpersonal relatedness and meaning between married partners.

Suggestion

Discuss with each other how *free you feel* to be yourself in each of these areas. *Please try not to blame your partner for your lack of freedom*, or tell your partner that he or she "should" or "should not" do this or that. The point of this exercise is to focus on these two important areas of *behav-*

ioral interaction in your marriage and talk about how free you feel to *be yourself with* your partner. Begin to question the validity of some of these NOT's.

Are there any masculine-feminine or husband-wife roles that are getting in the way of experiencing yourself fully in either of these two areas of the relationship?

Suggestion

Consider the maintenance needs first.

Discuss some of the marriage NOT's that you may be following. Remember that most of the maintenance needs NOT's are neither right or wrong. Many of them are simply *assumed* to be appropriate roles for husband and wife. Talk about the NOT's that you like to have and those that you don't really care for.

Freeing up some of the NOT's can not only help to "get the job done," but can be fun. The way this works best is to, once again, put the *relationship* into focus. Rather than assigning or assuming rigid guidelines for who does what around the house, many of the maintenance needs can be met by *both* partners as special *Relationship Contact Points*—or RCP's. That is, both partners can make an enjoyable experience out of things that "have" to be done. The aim is not so much to hurry up by helping each other to get the job done as it is an opportunity to play and communicate together.

Discuss for a moment the possibility of turning some of the marriage NOT's into more pleasurable relationship contact points, or RCP's.

Let's turn now to the affectional needs in marriage.

Special Person

By dividing the marriage relationship into these two areas couples are often surprised to find that most (if not all) of their behavioral interactions occur around "maintenance needs." The "affectional needs" are particularly important, however, because it is these behaviors which indicate that your partner is a *special person*. You probably let each other know this often early in your relationship but what about now?

Often partners remember each other as "special" people on special occasions—anniversary, birthday, Mother's Day-/Father's Day, etc. This may have started out as a fun spontaneous gesture, but for many these occasions have also turned into marriage NOT's. If my spouse really loved me he/she would NOT forget my birthday and certainly NOT our anniversary! Now rather than doing something special because you want to, you do it because you are expected to. And often under this demand situation, what you do is really not perceived as special or even desirable. We are reminded of the wife who said, "Every Valentine's Day he gives me a box of candy and I hate candy! Why doesn't he give me something I would appreciate?"

Communication in this area is also extremely important. We need information from our partner as to what makes him or her feel special. Calling your partner at the office might make him/her feel special. On the other hand, refraining from calling because you know what a busy schedule he/she has might be a very special personal gesture.

Suggestion

Sit facing each other and touch. Tell each other two things that you have done recently to let your partner know that he/she is a special person that is loved. Communicate specific behaviors:

"I picked a flower from the yard and gave it to you."

"I called you from the office to tell you that I was thinking of you."

"I told you how great you looked."

"I brought a surprise gift home to you." etc.

These "special person" behaviors can be meaningful and fun to do. This is a part of the circle of intimacy. Marriage takes creativity, planning, and *doing*. It is the behaviors that count. If you had trouble thinking about specific "special person" behaviors that you have done lately do not be discouraged. Just start now. It takes a little creativity, communication and following through. Tell each other two things that would make you feel special.

Touch Opportunities

One way to be free enough to enjoy the playful side of physical intimacy is to develop and maintain an open communication about pleasures and preferences. In other words to feel free enough to communicate (verbally and nonverbally) what you would like to experience more or less on a moment-by-moment basis. Remember we are changing people. We may want to touch or be touched in different ways at different times.

Because of this, open lines of communication with I-messages are essential. This also means that each of us has the responsibility of forming our own opinion about our likes and dislikes. If you are to be authentic with each other, you must feel free to explore a variety of intimate situations with each other. If you find from *your own experience* that you do not like to touch or be touched in a certain way then move on to something else—for the time being.

In other words, if you have never touched a certain place on you or your partner, or experienced a certain sensation, or done a certain thing with your partner, then you are probably not allowing yourself to form your own opinion. Denying yourself of the opportunity of forming your own opinion because you grew up believing that certain things shared between married partners was "bad" or "perverted" is not discovering anything about you—a unique person and partner in a unique relationship. Too many NOT's can tie up intimacy in marriage. If there are any "prescribed guidelines," let it be that each marriage relationship can freely evaluate its own personally rewarding meaningful and growth-producing "standards."

Suggestion

Below there is a list of various potentially intimate activities. We would like you to go through the entire list one item at a time and discuss if you would like to experience more or less of these activities together. Some of the terms are purposefully vague. This may give you the opportunity of interpreting what this means to you. You may find that you may want to try something more while your partner wants to experience it less. If so, be very clear what each other means by the particular activity in question. Can you help each other arrive at a satisfactory solution?

___ Bathing each other
___ Kissing
___ Aggressiveness: By self___ By partner___
___ Variety of time or place for touch opportunities
___ Variety of positions for intercourse
___ Sharing sexual fantasies
___ Washing each other's hair
___ Foot caressing
___ Body caressing
___ Anal Stimulation
___ Genital caresses without leading to intercourse
___ Talking during lovemaking
___ Tenderness
___ Manual stimulation of partner
___ Manual stimulation by partner
___ Use of accessories (vibrators, mirrors, lotions, etc.)
___ Frequency of intercourse
___ Oral stimulation by partner
___ Oral stimulation of partner
___ Quickies
___ Touching and warmth after intercourse
___ Breast caressing
___ Orgasms
___ Spontaneity
___ Freedom to explore each other physically
___ Communication about sexual attitudes and feelings on a moment-by-moment basis
___ Fun and laughter
___ Seductiveness: By self___ By partner___
___ Interplay

Being free offers us the opportunity of being with each other in the present. This may be a new dimension of togetherness because quite often concerns of the future and particularly of the past do not allow relating in the present. Being free then is exploring the present fully with your partner without limiting your actions and behaviors because of what happened in the past or what might happen in the future. The idea of relating in the present can be a very dramatic concept which permits change and, consequently, discovery to occur. It says in effect that you cannot predict your behavior or your partner's behavior based upon historical events. Being free to put the past where it belongs—behind you—means that you are free to let the present become an important part of you and your relationship. This is particularly true where intimacy is concerned. Intimacy is created by *two* people who are free enough to let this meaningful process evolve between them. The growing edge of intimacy is discovery. This means building upon the present moment. This we can control and are a part of. The past is gone forever and there is nothing we can do to change it. We learn from the present and we miss a valuable opportunity of learning something new about ourself and our partner when we confuse learning with "knowing."

Suggestion

Take turns giving each other a breast and genital caress. No matter what has happened before in your relationship when genitals were touched, we suggest you take this experience as something new, something very special where you have the freedom to explore and relate in the present. The circle of intimacy offers you a wide variety of special behaviors and feelings that can be explored with your partner. A genital caress can be one way and intercourse can be another. One does not necessarily and invariably have to follow the other. Learning this can open up a tremendous amount of intimate pleasure between partners. Genital caresses can be appreciated in and of themselves just for what they are if we allow ourselves the freedom to explore and not search. In other words, give this touch opportunity all of the attention you can without thinking "foreplay" or "here we go up the ladder again," etc.

Sex is what you think it is. Whatever that might be we suggest that sex is more than something done to or for a partner, penis-in-vagina, having orgasms, just routine, a guessing game, a matter of timing or erection-penetration-ejaculation. Sex is fun, a natural function, and a form of communication.

You may want to include a body caress with the genital and breast caress. When you begin the genital caress, touch inside your partner's thighs, moving up, around and over the buttocks onto the small of the back. Spend some time with the thighs. Give each other information ("I like what you are doing," "A little softer there," etc.)

Repeat each stroke several times.
Use your forearms with the same movements.
Turn over.
Follow the same procedure, using your hands inside the thighs, *around* the genitalia, up to the navel.
Lightly touch the nipples and the tissue around the breast.
Play with the breast and nipples.
Repeat several times.
Use a nonallergenic lotion for the genital caress.
Gently caress his penis/her clitoris.
Take the attitude that this organ is *yours* to enjoy and play with.
Learn what feels good to your partner—the right amount of pressure and movement. Your partner can give you important information with I-messages and I-movements.
Gently stroke the entire genital area. Focus on the feelings you are receiving from your hands.
Use both hands. Experiment. Play. Talk with each other.

Communicate either verbally or nonverbally about what you would like more of or what feels sensitive or irritating. Find things that are enjoyable to you and enjoyable for your partner. Are there some areas that are more sensitive or pleasurable than other areas. Don't work for anything to happen. Nothing is supposed to. Having an erection, lubricating, or orgasm is not the *goal*. They may happen. They may not. Getting ready for RT is not the purpose of this experience.

Play and explore—don't demand or expect. This is not *foreplay* but *intimate* play.

A part of loving is sharing intimate feeling—of just being with the person you love—of just playing—having fun—learning—appreciating.

Learn about each other's bodies. Knowing as much as you can helps you to understand, and appreciate, and care.

You may want to relax together for a while and just lie close or talk and resume genital stroking in a few minutes. Laughing, talking, stroking, and relaxing are all a part of intimacy.

Show each other ________________ communicate
Teach each other ________________ learn
Learn together ________________ it's the only way
Take your time ________________ experience the many,
many different ways of
sharing intimacy.

Chapter 20

Being Secure

What is Being Secure? Being secure with yourself as a partner and being secure with yourself as a person. Are the two different?
In what ways are you different from you as a person and you as a partner?
Is the real you often expressed more to others rather than with your married partner?
Do you find saying "no" or saying "yes" easier outside or inside the marriage?
Do you think your partner feels more secure to be himself or herself inside or outside the marriage relationship?

Rules

Being secure has many meanings: to be free from care, anxiety, fear; to be confident, certain. These are just a few of the meanings of "being secure." These meanings when applied to vitalizing intimacy in marriage suggest that the partners arrived at some "rules" for themselves and their relationship which, if followed, will make them feel secure.

Frequently, however these "rules" are implicit. Seldom have the partners shared their thoughts and feelings on issues and/or behaviors and arrived at an agreeable "rule" that both believe would be beneficial to them and to their relationship.

Suggestion

Independently of each other take as much time as you need to list the current "rules" of your relationship. Make two lists—one for agreed upon rules and one for implicit rules. Be specific.

When you have finished your lists, think about the following:

1. Do I follow these rules? Does my partner?
2. Am I comfortable with them?
3. How and why did these rules come to be?
4. Are there some I would like to add or take away?
5. Are the implicit rules important enough to me to let my partner know?
6. How would I feel if I discovered my rules were foreign to my partner?

Sometimes we set rules to follow in our effort to feel secure. They give us objective criterion on which to base our security, our trust, and even our love. If our partner breaks a rule, even an implicit one, we have proof that he/she cannot be trusted, does not really love us, and we therefore feel insecure. This type of rule-setting is destructive.

Rules are not made to be broken, but they too may need to be allowed to change. As you grow and change so may your "rules."

Now, look at your lists again and select only those that you feel right now are absolutely essential to your happiness in your *relationship*. Share these with each other. Be Aware. Be Authentic. Be Free. Be Secure. This is trusting.

It is both trusting your own desires and feelings and trusting that your partner really wants to know what is important to you. Trust is an important feeling to have in the marriage. Distrust brings on feelings of not being secure, of not being able to be yourself with your partner.

Part of trust is learning to trust ourselves and the experiences that we have. As we develop more trust of the creative process within ourselves, we begin to accept our own feelings, and live by values which we can discover within ourselves. Only then can we begin to feel secure in expressing ourselves in our own unique way. Becoming oneself *in* the relationship is one of the most rewarding aspects of the marital relationship. This is the process of becoming a *real* member of the partnership.

Since a marriage partnership is made up of two different people, we will have our differences and our similarities. Problems often arise because some spouses have not learned to appreciate their partner's differentness and so they continuously try to manipulate, educate, reform, counsel and change the other person into his or her own liking (or image). This rarely if ever works, except to create "manipulator" and "manipulated" feelings. Many of us are perhaps unaware of the tremendous pressure we as "manipulators" tend to put on our wives, our husbands, and our children, to have the same feelings and ideas that we do.

In an intimate relationship, there is a willingness for the other person to have different feelings, different values, and different goals. In other words, there is a willingness for him or her to be a separate person. As we become more willing to be ourself, we will more readily encourage our partner to be himself/herself.

What better definition of love is there than two people who are working on their own growth and potential *with* each other? This is the process of growing individually together in the marriage. By becoming a part of our partner's growth we are creating intimacy in the relationship.

Suggestion

Discuss for a moment the idea that you are creating intimacy in the relationship by *becoming a part of your partner's growth.*

How can you help your partner become the total person that he or she wants to become in the relationship? How can you help each other become the person you would like to become when you are away from the relationship?

Time Out

Part of being secure is also being separate. Each of us has our own personal need for privacy. A part of intimacy is learning to respect our own *and* our partner's domain. There is a need at times to be alone and separate from the relationship. We call this "time out." It does not mean leaving the relationship because of problems or because you are angry with your partner. It really means a time to be alone to think, to plan, or just to be.

This might mean:

Going to a separate room in the house.
Taking a drive or a walk.
Working on a hobby.

We are not talking about separateness because of "work" or because of scheduled activities or because "Friday night is my night out." Time out is time alone.

Suggestion

Discuss for a moment this concept of "time out." Is it threatening for you? What can you or your partner do to make you feel more comfortable with it? Would you like some "time out"?

Transition Period

A special "time out" that has been particularly meaningful to couples is taken when the partner returns home at the end of the day. Rather than being met with problems ("The air-conditioner is on the blink," or "Mary needs braces," or "Johnny got into a fight"), the partner is met with a Special Person behavior (a full body hug, or "I love you," or a love-note on his/her favorite chair). This is only the beginning of the "transition period." After having been greeted in this way, the returning partner then takes as much "time out" as is needed to unwind from the day's work before attempting time-*in*. The amount of time-out needed varies with individuals and with the same individual on different occasions (5 minutes—2 hours). The preferred way of spending time out also varies (reading the paper, watching the news, taking a shower). But one thing seems to hold constant—this Transition Period allows time-*in* to be quality time. You may not have as many minutes or hours together in an evening, but the time you do have together is really *together*.

There are situations where this Special Person greeting with "time out" is not possible (for example, both partners work outside the home and return together or one partner's exclusive job is homemaker) but, even so, a transition period of some type is important.

Suggestion

What type of Transition Period fits your situation? Do you need one? What would you like to have happen at the end of your working day?

Being secure also means representing yourself—using I-messages—giving your partner information and learning about your partner.

In *VIM* we have talked a lot about the three components of marriage. This is composed of the two unique partners and the unique partnership. Putting these three components in clear perspective can often be very helpful. It is not uncommon that partners feel unhappy or dissatisfied but do not know exactly why or what to do about it. The next suggestion may be very helpful in laying out some positive plans for you, your partner, and your relationship.

Suggestion

We would like each of you to make two separate lists. You might *each* write what these lists are at the top of two separate pieces of paper.

The first list is: I Want for Me. This would be a list of things that you think you would like to make *you* happy in your marriage.

The second list is: I Want for Us. This list is composed of those things that *you* think the relationship needs to make it a good one.

These are two very important lists. They deserve a lot of thought and time because they form the basis for positive change in a growing partnership.

You may want to think about this list for the next day or so. In any event, make up your lists separately without discussing them. It is very important to try to be as specific as you can. For example, stay away from statements like "I would like to be a better person" or "I think the relationship should always be a happy one." In other words, rather than saying "I would be happier if we would communicate more" say something like "I would be happier if we would spend 15 minutes a day over breakfast really communicating about our relationship."

When you have finished these lists then go over them together. Help each other clarify issues or revise the statements only if the understanding is not clear.

If you have been honest in making out these lists you should have some good ideas of what would make the Me-You-Us more meaningful.

Can you agree on one or two specifics from each person's lists to begin experiencing?

How can you help each other do this?

Date these lists. These lists will change. Hopefully, these lists can serve as a guide toward positive changes.

Business Meeting

Often it is necessary for married partners to agree on having a regularly scheduled "business meeting" to discuss the relationship and to update these lists. Considering the small amount of attention that the relationship receives because of all of the other demands that seem to have a higher priority, the "business meeting" can definitely be important—even essential—in reversing this pattern. The primary agenda for these meetings is the relationship. It is at these times that partners can share feelings, discuss priorities, and make special plans. This would not be the time to discuss the children or finances or anything else unless it is directly related to the relationship.

Suggestion

Marriage is a business. Do you think that a regular business meeting just for the two of you would be helpful? If so, decide on a time, perhaps once a week at first, and try it out for a few months. After this time you can talk over your feelings about the sessions and perhaps make additional changes.

Marriage is a process of exchanging vulnerabilities. Being secure is being vulnerable. Vulnerability is representing yourself in an open and authentic communication with your partner. One of the greatest features of being vulnerable is that it permits a personal openness to the discovery of self and partner.

Being secure also means being free to explore fully the Circles of Intimacy—all three circles (Special Person, Sensory, and Erotic). If you have followed the suggestions in *VIM* you have a good idea about the three circles of intimacy.

You have the opportunity in your marriage to create and expand your intimacy together. This, however, is very much up to you. Waiting around for your partner to do something first is playing a game. Intimacy is created and if you have experienced some positive insightful moments together as you have experienced *VIM* then you have probably started making intimacy work in your marriage. Indeed every day can be a beginning.

Suggestion

Love each other—intimately.

Index